TRIUMPH
2000

DEFINING THE SPORTING
SALOON

KEVIN WARRINGTON

AMBERLEY

First published 2016

Amberley Publishing
The Hill, Stroud,
Gloucestershire, GL5 4EP

www.amberley-books.com

ISBN: 978 1 4456 5563 5 (print)
ISBN: 978 1 4456 5564 2 (ebook)

British Library Cataloguing in Publication Data.
A catalogue record for this book is available from the British Library.

Typeset in 10pt on 13pt Celeste.
Typesetting by Amberley Publishing.
Printed in the UK.

Contents

1

Triumph: The Origins of a Brand

In 1885, at the age of twenty-two, an enthusiastic young German with a gift for languages arrived in London from Nuremburg to take up a position with Kelly and Company, which was compiling trade directories. His name was Siegfried Bettmann, and his career would lead him rapidly to working on his own account, first as a distributor of sewing machines, then moving quickly to the booming market for bicycles, naturally leading in due course to motorcycles and eventually motor cars. By coincidence, 1885 was the year in which a fellow German, Karl Benz, was to show the first internal combustion engine powered vehicle to the world. The business that Bettmann was to establish and develop would be given the name 'Triumph' and would through the twentieth century become one of the most respected names for both motorcycles and cars.

Six months after arriving in London, Bettmann had resigned his position with Kelly to become the representative for overseas countries with the White Sewing Machine Company of Cleveland, Ohio. Following a disagreement with his manager, George Sawyer, a name that will recur in the story very soon, Bettmann left this employment and set up his own business, S. Bettmann and Company, as a representative for manufacturing companies located in his native country. This period saw a huge interest in cycling, both as a leisure activity and as a means of basic transport. Identifying the humble bike as a product with potential, Bettmann arranged for the established Birmingham company of William Andrews to design a machine for S. Bettmann and Company to sell both at home and abroad. A brand name for the cycles was needed, and the name 'Triumph' was chosen; a brand name that continues to this day, although now under completely different ownership.

Two years after Bettmann had arrived in London, he was joined by a fellow citizen from Nuremberg, Mauritz Shultz. The business relocated to Coventry, by then an emerging centre for the production of bicycles and in time to be a major manufacturing location for cars; the interests in the other products that had allowed Bettmann to establish his business were quietly forgotten. A third former Nuremberg resident Philip Schloss ran an office in London for Triumph, investing his entire wealth of £100 into the venture. In 1897, Triumph was incorporated as a Limited Company. The directors, including the original three partners in the business, were joined by the Mayor of Coventry and landlord of the premises that the company utilised, Alderman Tomson, a financier by the name of Friedlander and, despite the disagreement from twelve years previously, Bettmann's former manager from the White Sewing Machine Company, George Sawyer, was appointed Chairman.

Thus, the Triumph Cycle Company was to join the ever growing number of bicycle manufacturers, some of which were to evolve in the course of time into internal combustion powered vehicles, but most of which would be either taken over or fade away completely. In the case of Triumph, the path of the business was anything but smooth. Although the business was brisk, margins were slim, setting a pattern that was to follow the business for all of its life, and cash was tight. However, the involvement by the Dunlop Tyre Company through Irish businessman and financier Harvey du Cros had a positive impact on the young business's fortunes, leading to a rapid increase in sales outlets and the company's shares being offered to the public.

Early Triumph Motor Vehicles

While Bettmann was quite content with the cycle business, Shultz saw an opportunity with the new-fangled motorcycle; after several false starts, the first Triumph motorbike was developed in 1902, using a strengthened bicycle frame fitted with a bought-in engine. Three years later, a new machine was introduced being entirely of Triumph design. Success in competitions came immediately, particularly in the Isle of Man TT event where Triumph machines appeared regularly in the list of class winning if not outright winning machines.

The year 1914 brought turmoil with the outbreak of the First World War. For Bettmann personally as a notable figure of German birth, life became particularly uncomfortable. Since setting up business in Coventry, Bettmann had fully involved himself in the affairs of his adopted country becoming Mayor of Coventry in 1913. He was subjected to an unfounded attack on his personal integrity by a national newspaper that had accused him of sending company profits back to Germany and was fortunate not to be interned as an alien. However, he was forced to resign as Mayor and from several company directorships, including one with the Standard Motor Company. On the business front, events took an interesting direction with Triumph becoming a primary supplier of motorcycles to the Army: the model 'H', otherwise known by the forces as the 'Trusty Triumph'.

Following the Armistice, Triumph was to move into the car business in 1923 with a range of quite orthodox models, and in 1927, a 7 hp model was announced and marketed as the Triumph Super Seven. This competed with the more famous Austin 7 model and was similar in many respects except that the Triumph was more expensive reflecting the higher standard of finish. In 1933, Triumph appointed Donald Healey as 'experimental manager', a successful rally driver, who was to become famous in his own right for his own range of cars that would compete much later with Triumph. Healey's motor sport adventures and 'Boys' Own' exploits brought welcome publicity to the company, and the product range was extended during the 1930s to include a particularly attractive range of full-size cars sold as the Dolomite and Gloria. One very distinctive design feature of Triumph's cars in this period was the 'waterfall' grille, something that did not meet the wholehearted approval of

An early motor car from the Triumph brand, the Super Seven.

The original Triumph Dolomite of the 1930s featured a highly stylised radiator grille that was very much in the art deco style of the period.

For customers looking for a less-flamboyant style, a simpler radiator style was also offered.

the market being a little too adventurous for some of the customers that Triumph needed to attract to remain successful. For these customers, a similar car but with a conventional radiator grille was offered as the Vitesse. Those familiar with Triumph cars of more recent years will note the origin of the model names that were to be used again on Triumph cars during the 1960s and 1970s.

The economic recession of the 1930s claimed numerous car companies with many either ceasing to trade or being taken over by larger companies. Particularly in Coventry, many of the smaller businesses were acquired by the Rootes Brothers into their growing empire of businesses, but Triumph retained its independence. Throughout the 1930s, disposals were made commencing in 1932 when the original bicycle business was sold followed in 1936 with the sale of the motorcycle business. Car production continued until the outbreak of World War again in 1939 when Triumph's works were turned over to aircraft engine manufacturing. With debts of some £150,000, it was not to be long before the company's bankers called in receivers, and the business was sold to a manufacturing conglomerate, Thomas W. Ward & Company.

By the time peace came again in 1945, there was nothing of the Triumph company left, other than the name. Coventry had been bombed savagely during the hostilities resulting in the complete destruction of the car manufacturing premises. Although Donald Healey had remained with Triumph and had already developed plans for a post-war range of cars, these did not meet with the approval of the current owners, so Healey and Messrs Ward were to part company. Essentially, all that remained of the Triumph business was the company name and the goodwill. At that time, the British motor industry was dominated by six large companies, called collectively (and with little imagination) 'the big six'. These comprised the Nuffield Group formed by William Morris, Austin, Ford, Vauxhall, the Rootes Group and the Standard Motor Company. Of these, the first four had no interest in acquiring a trade name with no collateral, the Rootes empire already included marques with similar characteristics to Triumph, but Standard in the form of its mercurial General Manager Sir John Black did express interest.

Standard, another Coventry-based company, had been building a traditional range of cars since the early years of the century. In addition to building its own cars, the company supplied major assemblies to other businesses, including Morgan and SS-Cars, which would shortly rename itself as Jaguar. With a plan to develop cars with more sporting pedigree, the remains of the Triumph company were of interest to Standard, and the business that was to become known as Standard-Triumph was formed in 1945. Of course, there had been little or no development of cars during the period of hostilities, so the first cars to return to the market in the late 1940s were those that had been on sale in 1939. With the Triumph factory and all the tooling destroyed, these cars were from the Standard model range. New models with the Triumph badge reappeared in 1949, finished in what is described as 'razor edge' coachwork – a style that had been popular with bespoke coachbuilders in the 1930s and which was greatly favoured by Black, lending a distinctly upmarket appearance to the car. Coincident with the new Triumph model, the Standard Vanguard was also announced, a car that was heavily influenced by US design. The Vanguard was an exceptionally sturdy car and sold well in export markets, an important factor during the early post-war years.

Standard ended production of Renown in 1954, but the Vanguard was to continue in production to be the final car model to be sold under the Standard name. With a

The Standard Motor Company had a reputation for solid, reliable cars that lived up to the branding of being 'the Standard' to which other manufacturers aspired. The cars of the late 1930s and immediate post-war years prior to the new designs going into production were similar in appearance to those produced by Morris and Ford, especially this Standard 8.

This 1936 'Flying Heavy Twelve' shows a style that is distinctly different to the styling of other cars despite retaining the general layout and six-light design of the era.

A collection of three Triumph Renown saloon cars show off the 'razor edge' styling so much liked by Sir John Black. Photographed in front of a Vickers VC-10 at the Brooklands Museum, Surrey.

The Standard Vanguard was to prove a reliable foreign currency earner during the immediate post-war austerity years. With its very distinctive transatlantic design, allegedly body stylist Walter Belgrove was dispatched to London to study cars outside the US Embassy to pick up the design features for this model.

production range stretching from 1947 until 1963, the last Vanguards bore little in common with the early cars other than name. Furthermore, the use of the word 'standard' had changed over the years from meaning at the forefront of design to inferring a sense of being quite ordinary with there being numerous apocryphal stories of potential customers, particularly in the United States, being interested in the car, but asking if perhaps a 'de luxe' version might be available.

During the 1950s, following the end of production of the Renown, the Triumph name was used on a small two-door saloon with similar styling to the Renown sold as the Triumph Mayflower, but until the announcement of the Herald in 1959, the brand name was limited to the TR range of sports car. One exception being in the United States where the little Standard 10 car was badged as a TR10, although it did not sell in large numbers. From 1963, all cars produced by Standard-Triumph would be sold as Triumphs, and the name of Standard, first used on a motor car in 1903, would be allowed to quietly fade away. However, it was not until 1970 that a formal announcement that Standard-Triumph, by now part of the British Leyland empire, would henceforth be formally known as the Triumph Motor Company. Despite the end of the Standard name by the Coventry business, the name continued to be applied to later British Leyland cars built under licence in India.

The razor edge styling of the Triumph Mayflower does not suit the smaller car in the way that it gave the earlier Renown a quality air. Mayflowers were intended as another car to be exported in large numbers to the United States, but volumes fell far short of expectations.

Following the limited success of the Mayflower, the next saloon car to carry the Triumph name was to be the Herald, a car that was to be very successful for the Coventry company, owing much to its distinctive Italian styling penned by Standard-Triumph's preferred stylist of the era, Giovanni Michelotti. This early coupé model is seen among a display of Triumphs.

2

The Triumph 2000

Today's car market is neatly divided into 'segments', defined on who the perceived customer might be. In the mid-1950s, the situation was less clear-cut. A small family car at the time might be a Morris Minor or Austin A35, and a large family car perhaps a Vauxhall Victor or Morris Oxford. The affluent would look towards the more prestigious brands such as Wolseley or Riley, while the professional business user would look for a car with an engine of 3-litres capacity, perhaps a Rover or a Jaguar. High performance was in general limited to small two-seater sports cars, an area where Triumph was enjoying great success, and the combination of sporting performance, good handling and room to carry a family was a market addressed only by a very few specialist manufacturers with pricing beyond the possibility of the typical owner. Things changed a little in the second half of the 1950s with the announcement by Jaguar of the 2.4-litre saloon, although an engine capacity of this size and the list price really took the car closer to the segment occupied by the 3-litre cars.

Typical of the small family car to be seen on the roads of Great Britain during the late 1950s and early 1960s is the ubiquitous Morris Minor, seen here driving through the grounds of the National Motor Museum at Beaulieu on a normal English summer's day.

Jaguar's smaller saloon cars of the 1950s and 1960s predated the market that was to be developed by Triumph, although the pricing was at a premium when compared to that asked by Triumph. Shown here is a Mark 2 model, a car that was to gain a slightly undesirable reputation as being the 'get away' car of choice for armed robbers.

With the Vanguard model now becoming a little tired, moves were underway to produce a completely new model to supplant it. With the market for cars booming at the time, the new car was to be as adventurous as the old car was traditional. Various advanced ideas were considered, including front wheel drive and pneumatic suspension, perhaps influenced by the newly introduced Citroën DS. Instead, the new design code-named 'Zebu' under the guiding hand of Chief Engineer Harry Webster settled on a design for a mid-sized car with class-leading performance and suspension. Unusually, the car would be built on a traditional chassis, featuring a transaxle transmission system. The body style was adventurous with pillarless doors and a reverse rake rear window. From certain viewing angles, the car exhibited a similar appearance to the yet–to-be-announced Ford 105E Anglia, although the Triumph was overall larger and a four-door model. Ford would themselves introduce a larger four-door model with similar design features to the Anglia in 1961 as the Consul Classic, a car that would be remarkably similar to 'Zebu' in appearance.

Everything would likely have proceeded as planned had a chance encounter with a visiting journalist to the Standard-Triumph design studios not informed Webster's team that another, then unspecified, British car manufacturer was working on a design with many of the same characteristics as the Triumph and that it would be on sale some years ahead. Worries also arose over the unconventional transmission leading to the project taking a lower priority.

Very rapidly, Standard-Triumph's finances took a downward turn, and a simpler solution to the issue of the Vanguard replacement model was considered. Project 'Zebu' was resurrected, but now with a conventional transmission and a body style that resembled a stretched version of the new Herald, but with four doors. While the Herald was a very stylish and up-to-date design, its transformation into the new 'Zebu', despite the involvement of Italian maestro Giovanni Michelotti, failed to capture the imagination of the higher levels of management at Standard-Triumph, and the exercise proceeded no further.

By 1960, the Vanguard remained as Standard-Triumph's large saloon car and was now into its third restyling. By this time, Michelotti had become involved in the redesign, but even his skill left the Vanguard as a rather staid design. Both saloons and estate models were available, and duo-tone colour schemes had become very fashionable. The final model in the range would be the Vanguard Six in which the new six-cylinder 2-litre engine would make its debut.

In the background, the financial situation at Standard-Triumph became even worse and had it not been for the ambitions of the Leyland Motor Company to gain a position in the car business, it is quite likely that Standard-Triumph would have disappeared. In May 1961, Leyland took full control of Standard-Triumph and, despite the perilous state of the finances, a programme of new model development was approved, including the resurrection of plans to replace the Vanguard model, now code-named 'Barb'. The final iteration of the company's large car, even as the Vanguard Luxury Six when fitted with the new six-cylinder engine that would eventually find its way into the replacement model, was outclassed by its competition, and sales were few and far between (only large orders of basic 'Ensign' models as staff cars for the Royal Air Force really keeping production alive).

A low-volume model of the Vanguard was sold as the 'Sportsman' with a revised front grill being a distinctive feature. There were discussions on launching this model under the Triumph brand with the trademark Triumph globe emblem making an appearance on the grille.

The Standard Ensign, an example of which being this estate car model shown at a TR Register event in 2013, was bought in large numbers by the United Kingdom's Royal Air Force and Royal Navy, helping to keep production going pending arrival of the new model.

Project 'Barb' was undertaken to a remarkably tight schedule. Design proposals were worked on by Michelotti in Turin and by Les Moore in Coventry with the mechanical elements of the vehicle under the direction of Harry Webster. Proposals were reviewed in the autumn of 1961, and the plan was to announce and show the new model at the 1963 Earls Court London Motor Show. Within two years, a completely new car would be developed and introduced with just the six-cylinder engine and gearbox being assemblies used elsewhere within the product range, everything else being designed from scratch. Returning to a monocoque design, the pressings and body shell assembly were completed by Pressed Steel Company, and completed assemblies were transported from the pressing plant at Swindon to Canley for final assembly.

To provide a comfortable ride in keeping with the market positioning of the new car, Triumph specified MacPherson struts for the front and independent rear suspension utilising coil springs and semi-trailing arms. This same rear suspension arrangement would later be used on the TR4A. Originally, the semi-trailing arms were intended to be mounted directly to the floor of the car until testing revealed unacceptable levels of vibration. A redesign to improve the ambience of the car resulted in the adoption of cast aluminium suspension arms to replace the original pressed steel items, now mounted on a rear subframe that also provided location for the differential. From the differential, the drive was taken via telescopic shafts to the rear hubs. Vertical movements in the rear wheels would cause the length of the drive shafts to vary with the telescoping being provided by simple splines, lubricated by grease and protected from dirt ingress by rubber sleeves. In time, and with significant mileage accumulated on the car, drivers found that the splines could develop a tendency to stick, thus temporarily varying the rear suspension geometry that would suddenly rectify itself giving rise to a phenomenon known by owners as the 'Triumph Twitch'.

An option of an overdrive unit was offered, along with a three-speed automatic transmission, although early deliveries were exclusively manual cars. In keeping with the age, a rack and pinion steering system was specified, but power assistance was not available at this stage, a feature that would be noticed in its lacking by the motoring

Above and opposite above: In 1962, Pressed Steel Company provided a quotation for the tooling and pressing of the body panels for the new Triumph car. As part of this quotation, a series of General Assembly drawings was produced, which formed part of the actual quotation as delivered to Standard-Triumph. These three extracts show the frontal and rear images of the body shell and major assemblies. The original drawings form part of the archive of the Triumph 2000 / 2500 / 2.5 Register, to whom they were donated after being found in a skip following demolition of the Works at Canley. (Triumph 2000 Register Limited Archive)

Opposite below: Triumph picked out certain features of the new car that were emphasised in the marketing brochure at the launch of the car. The arrangement for the independent rear suspension, the standard fit disc brakes, side repeater lamps for the turn signals and childproof locks were all features highlighted. (©BMIHT)

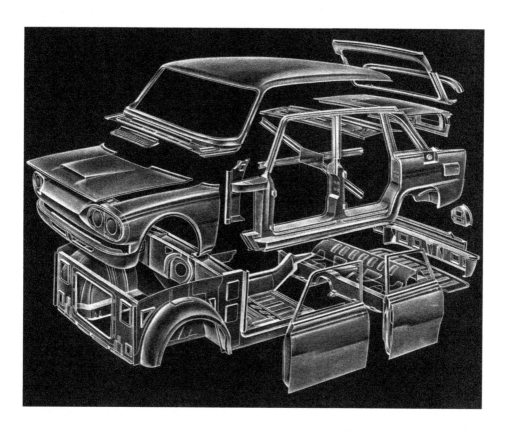

Independent rear suspension on the Triumph 2000. The system uses semi-trailing arms and coil springs with direct-acting hydraulic dampers.

Front disc brakes ensure safe, straight-line stops — no wet drums, no fading. The Triumph 2000 has stopping power to match its performance.

The Triumph 2000 is kind to rear-seat passengers. Ample leg room — and their own fresh-air and heater ducts, mounted behind the front seats.

Neat piano key switches control lights, wipers and windscreen washers. Easy to find, easy to operate (like all the controls on a Triumph 2000).

Evidence of the thought that has gone into every detail of the Triumph 2000 — all doors have child-proof locks. Toddlers are safe. You relax.

Twin reversing lights are built into the Triumph 2000. Another 'extra' you get for the basic price of this very fully equipped car.

Relay direction indicator flashers on the door pillars tell other drivers your intentions — even if they are right alongside the Triumph 2000.

Elegant functional design on a Triumph 2000. Twin headlamps, deeply recessed out of harm's way. Wrap-around front bumpers and flashers.

journalists of the day whose only criticism of the car would be its heavy steering. Braking was by rear drums and front discs, servo assisted.

The body style set a vision that would be common to all Triumph cars until production ended. A long front-hinged bonnet, a bright cabin section with thin pillars and a relatively short overhang luggage boot quickly became recognisable as the Triumph style. Four headlights were a design feature, something usually seen only on cars carrying a much higher price tag.

Inside the car, the owner was greeted with a level of style and comfort that would be expected from a level above that into which the 2000 was to be pitched. There was adequate space for five people, leather seating was an option, although the standard offering of vinyl was of such a good quality that it is even today often mistaken for hide, and the

Very early cars featured a two-tone dashboard covering that in certain colours was attractive, but could be quite garish with bolder colours. The original instruments used black figures on a white background. At this time, the steering wheel was a simple design with a central Triumph logo, repeated in script on the central cubby hole. Piano switches on either side of the instrument binnacle operated lights, wipers and the screen washer. One unusual feature of the Mark 1 model was the location of the indicator switch, which was operated by the driver's left hand. (Steve Parkin)

vision of quality was heightened by the presence of polished real wood door cappings and dashboard panels. An effective variable speed heating and demisting system was fitted as standard, and there was provision for a radio.

With so much being designed newly for the car, it was inevitable that mechanical assemblies would be ready ahead of the body shells. To allow for testing, an ingenious test rig was constructed from a prototype floor pan fitted with running gear and bodywork constructed from lengths of angle iron and tubular steel. Not surprisingly, this became known as the 'Birdcage' and was a regular sight around the West Midlands and Cotswold test routes.

The 2000cc six-cylinder engine was also engineered as a 1600cc unit seen in the company's 'Vitesse' small saloon, and product planning thoughts extended to fitting this engine into a less luxuriously equipped 'Barb' to create the Triumph 1600. Only one such pre-production Triumph 1600 was built. The decision being made to focus entirely on the 2000cc model, particularly as it had become clear that the rival Rover Company was planning on launching their own 2000cc model into the same market segment as the Triumph, and the cost differential between the two Triumphs and, presumably, the profit margins did not favour a two-model strategy.

The first official appearance of the new Triumph 2000 was to be at the London Motor Show, held as usual at Earls Court in October 1963, with the first retail customer deliveries for January 1964. However, Triumph had the foresight to supply forty early pre-production cars to identified target customers with two significant benefits: first, a real life appraisal of the car with the ability to identify any weaknesses that could be rectified prior to volume shipment, and second, to provide Triumph and especially the new car with welcome publicity ahead of its general availability.

Although this particular car dates from 1967, it exemplifies the style and design of the new Triumph. Even today, more than fifty years after it was first introduced, the sharp, sporting style and clean lines create an attractive design.

3

The Triumph 2000
Comes to Market

Just one week before Triumph formally announced the 2000, the Rover Company launched its own 2000 model, code-named the P6. The Rover was also a car of distinctive style with numerous advanced features, not least of which was a body design featuring panels mounted onto a unit frame in a style reminiscent of the Citroën DS, launched some eight years earlier. Again, with all round independent suspension, a stylish interior and 2-litre power, the cars were conceptually very similar. At the rear, the Rover utilised a de Dion rear axle and inboard rear disc brakes, and at the front, the coil springs were rotated through 90 degrees longitudinally under the front wings with movements transmitted via bell cranks. This provided for a wide engine compartment with the possibility of installing Rover's gas turbine technology at some future time. Both cars provided luxurious seating, but while the Triumph could comfortably transport five people, the Rover was limited to four with individual rear seats precluding the carriage of a fifth person.

Standard-Triumph's Vanguard saloon had become unfashionable at the end of its life, and that problem was shared across Warwickshire by the Rover Car Company whose P4 model range had also reached its sell by date. Worthy and solid, the car had earned itself the nickname of 'Auntie's Rover'.

Above: Rover's new 2000 was an equally stylish design that was to have a long production life remaining in production alongside its Triumph rival even when both companies became part of the British Leyland behemoth. This particular car with commission number 100 is a very early 1963 car that was selected by Rover to be one of the two cars to feature on its stand at the London Motor Show and subsequently to be shipped to New York for the launch of the model in the United States.

Right: Although this image shows a much later car, the interior layout between the first and last cars did not change, other than for the materials used for trimming and seat coverings. The Triumph provides ample space for three adults in the rear, and even with the front seats set for a large driver, leg room is more than sufficient.

Conversely, the Rover 2000 was fitted with armchair shaped rear seats that limited the ability to carry a fifth passenger for anything other than the shortest distances.

The dashboard layout chosen by Rover also featured traditional wood with a wide shelf and rectangular binnacle containing the speedometer, temperature and fuel gauges. The speedometer worked on a moving-ribbon principle.

However, only the Triumph was initially available as a twin carburettor version, Rover customers would have to wait for the 2000TC, TC standing for twin carburettors, to be introduced in the UK market late in 1966, although a twin carburettor version of the Rover would be available for export markets earlier in that year. And of course, the Triumph had the cachet of a six-cylinder engine, something the Rover would never offer. Similarly, the Rover 2000 was not available with automatic transmission.

With the announcement of two significant models in the 2-litre class, the managements at Luton (Vauxhall), Dagenham (Ford), Longbridge (BMC) and locally in Coventry (Rootes Group) must have been most concerned. At a stroke, the middle management and business professional car buyer had not one but two new models featuring a standard of appointment that matched the features traditionally seen in the 3-litre class, both with up-to-the-minute but different styling. One of the models carried a brand image of traditional 'Britishness' (Rover) and the other of youthful sporting prowess (Triumph).

Triumph as a brand was renowned for its sporting models, particularly the TR, and more recently at the time of the announcement of the 2000, the new Spitfire and recently

The Triumph front-hinged bonnet opening to beyond vertical makes access to the engine bay simple. The tops of the suspension mounts can be seen, although a wide engine bay is still retained. Twin Zenith-Stromberg carburettors fuel the engine.

The Rover may only have four cylinders, but it does have an overhead cam rather than the Triumph's pushrod valve gear. Fuelling is by way of a single SU carburettor. The shape of the engine bay was designed to allow the possibility of Rover's jet turbine engine to be fitted, which of course was never fitted in a production car, but the space was to be very useful some years later when the Buick designed 3500 V8 engine was installed.

introduced Vitesse. With four doors, seating for five and a boot with ample storage for all the paraphernalia of a growing family, the new 2000 immediately became attractive to enthusiastic motorists who found themselves with family commitments that required more space and refinement than the two-door sports cars of their youth. Until the end of production, the big Triumph saloon continued to find a ready market among those who, however, reluctantly had found it necessary to move to a 'more sensible' form of motoring, but retain the driving qualities and performance of a sports car.

In the early 1960s, 2-litre engined cars in the market segment targeted by both Triumph and Rover were a bold move. Traditionally, rivals had powered their cars with engines of a nominal 1.5-litre capacity, stretching to 1725cc in the case of the Rootes Group models. Prior to the introduction of the Triumph 2000, a prospective customer looking at alternatives in the mid-market segment might consider models from Vauxhall, BMC or Rootes.

The Vauxhall dealer could propose the Victor FC, also a new introduction for 1964, but visually similar to the earlier FB model from 1961 and thus without the cachet of a genuine new model. Its 1594cc engine with four cylinders developed a quoted 70 bhp and had a list

Triumph's TR sports cars sold well from the 1950s to the end of the company's existence and retained a loyal customer following. When family responsibilities meant that the two-seater sports car could no longer carry all the paraphernalia necessary, Triumph offered the 2000 as a solution, retaining the brand imagery and driving style, but with a more practical four doors and seats.

General Motor's UK business of Vauxhall manufactured and sold the Victor as a large family/business saloon with styling that harked back to the 1950s. A higher performance and specification model was sold as the VX 4/90. (Clive Wilkin)

The interior of Vauxhall's VX4/90 went some way towards approaching the quality of the Triumph as this press release photograph issued by Vauxhall Motors Ltd shows. The range topping car has a floor gear change and pull up handbrake, unlike lower specification cars that used a column change and 'umbrella' parking brake. The dashboard layout is very transcontinental in appearance with an early appearance of fake wood. (Vauxhall Motors Ltd)

price of £647, including purchase tax, but a higher performance model equipped with an enhanced level of trim, the Victor VX 4/90 was quoted at 91 bhp, although the intending customer would need to find an additional £200 to drive away in this car.

Moving to the BMC dealers, the prospective customer first needed to decide on his sub-brand; despite the Austin and Nuffield organisations merging in 1952, brand loyalties remained firm, and with the rival dealer networks remaining intact, essentially the same badge engineered cars were sold by competing dealers frequently within walking distance of one another. Austin, Morris, Riley, MG and Wolseley all offered individual versions of the long-lasting 'Farina' model range, introduced in 1959 and finally ending production in 1971. By 1964, the car offered a 1.6-litre engine with either single or twin carburettors producing a quoted 61 bhp in the Austin rising up to 72 bhp in the Riley. Trim levels were minicab basic in the cheaper models, becoming comparable to the Triumph at the top of the range in the Wolseley and Riley, although the price demanded was in the region of £1,088.

Further along the road, the Rootes dealer might propose a Hillman Super Minx. The more prestigious Rootes marques would offer similar levels of refinement to the Triumph: a Humber Hawk perhaps? This offered an engine of 2267cc, although only four cylinders and a wood and leather interior that was the equal of the Triumph, and the price would be an attractive £1,057, including purchase tax, within a few pounds of the price demanded for the new Triumph model. Styling, while admittedly a matter of personal choice, looked backwards to the 1950s, and especially to the styles of Detroit rather than an adventurous up-to-the-minute outline.

What Did the Press Think?

Autocar carried an article in its issue of 18 October 1963, but this was just a detailed description of the new car, and the first full road test appeared in the rival magazine *Motor* in March 1964. Noting that the only item in the car to have been carried over from a previous model was the engine, the magazine began its review by commenting, '*The Triumph 2-litre engine is an outstanding feature of a generally excellent design.*' The handling came in for comment as well mentioning that '*respect for the Triumph grows gradually as you press it harder and find how well balanced it remains*' helped by a driving position that was said to be '*excellent*', but some features, particularly the organ stop style throttle pedal, came in for criticism. In Australia, the magazine *Wheels* was equally impressed and started their July 1964 review thus '*The term "a real driver's car" has been grossly overworked. In the case of the Triumph 2000 it is probably the understatement of the year. It is a marvellous automobile.*' Praise indeed.

Triumph 2000 Automatic

The summer of 1964 saw the introduction of the automatic transmission option utilising a Borg-Warner 35 epicyclic gearbox coupled to a torque convertor. Traditionally, the gear selector for two-pedal cars had been mounted on the steering column, often connected to the gearbox via cables, and such systems were frequently subject to adverse comment due to the vagueness of selection. Breaking completely with tradition, the gear selector for the

Triumph was floor mounted in the same position as the traditional manual change lever, working in a fore and aft plane. A test in *Modern Motor* magazine dated March 1965 was effusive in its praise of the new 2000 Automatic, ending the review by saying that *'the Triumph 2000 automatic is an exceptionally good motor car, providing a degree of refinement in design, engineering and finish which sets it apart from its competitors'*. The only demerit mentioned being the absorption of power through the automatic transmission reducing top speed on test to 84 mph.

Meanwhile, in the United States, the influential magazine *Road and Track* also tested a 2000 and commented that based on their own experience of the Borg-Warner 35 automatic gearbox it was *'better suited to the 2000's 6 cylinder engine than the engine of any other car in which we have encountered it'*.

The first year of production saw approximately 20,000 cars built with minor improvements to the design being made in early production. The most significant change was the mounting of the rear subframe based on early completion experience, but a series of Technical Service Notes was issued to dealers in the early production life of the car rectifying such issues as wheel-rim embellishers potentially chafing tyre valve stems, modifications to the fitting of the front brake flexible hydraulic hoses to prevent fouling of the tyre on full steering lock and full suspension travel and rectifications to eliminate squealing front disc brakes. All of these were dealt with on cars already delivered to customers by way of routine servicing and none were the subject of a manufacturer's recall.

The first significant change to the car would occur in the latter part of 1965.

The centrally mounted automatic transmission selector lever is shown here. Notice that this car is fitted with a later style Mark 1 steering wheel complete with chrome horn ring. The central cubby box houses a speaker for a car radio. (Steve Parkin)

Giovanni Michelotti had a reputation of being able to sketch a design in just a few minutes. This original Michelotti-signed sketch was displayed in the bar of a public house in Coventry prior to being donated to the Triumph 2000 / 2500 / 2.5 Register in 2013. The sketch shows many features that were used on the 2000: the radiator grille, bonnet shape and ventilator, the shape and form of the bumpers, and the strakes across the rear wheel arch and the front quarter sidelights and turn signals. The single headlights, though, are reminiscent of the later 'Ajax' design, also by Michelotti, which became the Triumph 1300. (Triumph 2000 Register Ltd Archive)

The reverse side of the sketch above shows the same design rendered as a colour image. (Triumph 2000 Register Ltd Archive)

4

An Upmarket Estate Car

Today, the estate car, wagon or brake, depending on location is seen as a 'lifestyle' vehicle. In the mid-1960s, the estate car was fundamentally a working vehicle targeted at, for example, the corner shop retailer, who might want to use a car type vehicle to visit the newly established 'cash and carry' rather than a commercial panel van, or the sales representative who needed a vehicle larger than the traditional saloon to haul sample goods or make deliveries. As such, estate cars were rather utilitarian and in some cases effectively small panel vans fitted with side windows and upholstered with a folding rear seat.

At a stroke, Triumph's introduction of the 2000 Estate changed the market. Now, the successful businessman could purchase a comfortable, well-trimmed and powerful estate car that was to the same specification as the saloon from which it was derived, but provided the facility to haul larger capacities of cargo than could be accommodated in a car boot. It was a car that was unique in the market and would continue to be so until it went out of production in 1977.

Triumph marketed the 2000 estate as a key part of the product range, as can be seen from the estate car appearing on the cover of the 1966 sales brochure. (©BMIHT)

Standard-Triumph had a long history of building estate cars, but prior to the 2000 being launched, they were rather utilitarian vehicles as this Standard Ten Companion model shows.

An early example of a 2000 estate being displayed at a classic car show by its enthusiastic owners who had travelled with the car from France for the event.

Accommodating the load carrying space required modification to the bodywork beyond the simple addition of sheet metalwork, new glazing and a tailgate. The saloon car had its fuel tank located across the rear of the car between the boot space and rear seat. This was to be moved to a new location under the rear floor of the estate load area and the spare wheel, which had previously been accommodated somewhat awkwardly in the boot, was now positioned horizontally alongside the fuel tank. The load space was accessed by a large single-piece part-glazed tailgate in the usual form seen today and unlike the then frequently used method of a split tailgate.

Estate car production was a complicated procedure. A quotation had been obtained from Pressed Steel Company for the pressing and construction of complete estate car bodies, but was not pursued due to the high cost with a figure in the region of half a million pounds quoted for tooling. With estate cars representing a relatively small share of the market, it was not unusual for the conversion to be undertaken by a specialist. Triumph's approach to assembling the 2000 estate car was to be different to that employed by the other volume car builders at the time in that partly built body shells were first shipped to the coach building concern of Carbodies where the estate bodies would be finished prior to shipping to Canley for completion. Carbodies were a long-established designer and builder of coachwork having entered the market in the 1920s as coachwork supplier to Alvis and MG and establishing an expertise in the conversion of mainstream saloon models to convertibles, but are best known as the manufacturer of the iconic London Taxi.

Carbodies' quote for tooling was a much more acceptable £75,000, but a downside to the method of construction to be adopted was that a significant amount of lead loading, approximately £120 per car, would be required to finish the bodywork. With the commodity price for lead being highly volatile at the time, an agreement was reached whereby the price paid by Triumph would be adjusted every three months in accordance with the cost of the lead supplies required. Initially, Triumph estimated that the market demand for an estate car would require a production of around twenty cars per week. Market acceptance meant that production rapidly rose to 100 cars per week with a total run over the entire model range approaching 22,000 cars.

The saloon car was blessed with a very deep boot, but at the expense of the spare wheel being carried upright and obliquely in the boot. The fuel tank is positioned between the boot and the back seat, so clearly both spare wheel and fuel tank location would need to be modified to create the estate car.

Right: Although the car illustrated is a Mark 2 estate car, the load area of the newer car was not changed. The large single-piece glazed tailgate suspended on torsion bars gave easy access to the load area that could be easily extended by folding the rear seats. The spare wheel and fuel tank are now under the carpeted false floor.

Below: Showing the assembly line for Triumph estate cars at Carbodies, these are later Mark 2 cars being built from partly assembled shells shipped from Pressed Steel Company. At the very front of the line, a number of the familiar FX4 London taxis can be seen confirming that this photograph was indeed taken at Carbodies. (Collection of Bill Munro)

A folding rear seat was fitted, the load space carpeted and fitted with aluminium rubbing strips and the polished wood cappings were continued to the full extent of the load space. An interesting styling feature was the adoption of opening quarter-light windows in the rearmost glass.

The estate car had some detail differences from its saloon underpinnings. Relocating the fuel tank resulted in a reduction from 14 gallons (63 litres) to 11.5 gallons (52 litres), and the fuel filler cap moved from the left side of the rear wing to the right, now being fitted with a single-piece combined flap and cap. The saloon continued to use a separate cap under a flap.

Performance was affected slightly. While the saloon would claim to complete the 0–60 mph benchmark in 13.6 seconds and go on to a maximum speed of 95 mph, the estate car would take 14.9 seconds to reach 60 mph and reported a slightly lower top speed of 92 mph. Both styles of car were available with the option of overdrive or an automatic transmission, and while radial tyres remained as an optional extra for the saloon, they were a standard fitting on the estate car.

Autocar tested an estate car for an issue published in November 1966 and were glowing in enthusiasm for the car commenting that the '*revised bodywork for the estate car at the rear is neatly done*' and avoided the appearance of being a conversion from a saloon. They found that the car felt '*extremely safe*', and the grip from the tyres was such that it mattered '*little whether the roads are wet or dry*'. One problem with the car was noted: great care was necessary when refuelling to prevent petrol being blown back through the filler, something that current owners of the cars will be familiar with.

Even with the rear seat raised, a substantial load could still be carried. The quality of the finish from the passenger cabin was continued into the load space.

Right: An interesting styling feature was the inclusion of an opening quarter-light window in the glazed load areas.

Below: The rear wings of an estate car started life as the same pressings as would be used to build a saloon model. Consequently, the point at which the rear C pillar was cut-off remains visible to close inspection on an estate car.

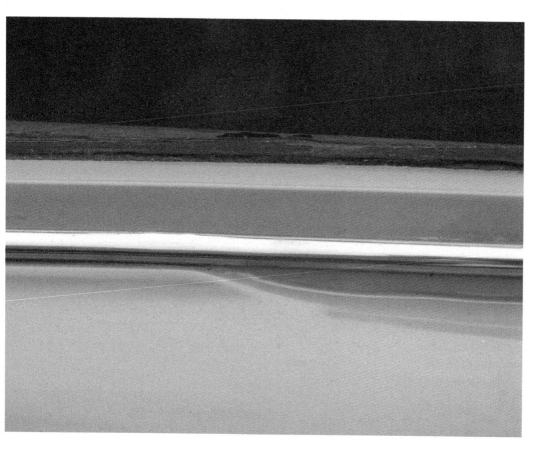

Many owners of the 2000 saloons who have driven off after closing the flush cover, but forgetting to first replace the fuel filler cap, will regret that Triumph chose to not fit the one-part cap as used on the estate. For owners who drove both saloon and estate models, the opportunity for embarrassment when refuelling was high – saloons and estates had their fuel fillers on opposite sides.

Improvements across the Range

With the new car selling well in the market, there was little need for much change to be made to the design, but a number of detail changes were made across the range. A revised ventilation system now provided a pair of rotatable vents in the lower dashboard coupled with extraction vents fitted in the rear window overhang of the saloon and at the waist level on the estate version tailgate. The claim for the first motor car to be fitted with full flow ventilation is often disputed, but Triumph was indisputably an early adopter of such a system with the 2000. Originally, a folding vanity mirror had been fitted inside the glovebox, mounted on the inside of the cover. This moved to the more conventional location behind the passenger side sun visor, a new style of horn control was fitted now using a central bar and full diameter ring and changes were made to the main instruments, which were now black faced with white markings, an inversion of the original design. Most notably, the original two-colour dashboard was substituted with one finished in a single colour.

However, the traditional estate car was not the only line of thought at the time. A prototype 'fastback' car was also developed as a styling exercise, but was not put into production. Pre-dating by some years the trend towards 'hatchback' cars and with some styling cues that were later adopted in the Rover 3500 SD1, ironically the very model that was to replace both the Triumph 2000 and Rover P6 ranges, the car featured an extremely large glazed tailgate sloping from the roofline to the top of the rear light clusters. The tailgate was exceptionally heavy and load carrying space quite limited. Prior to the adoption of gas struts to hold top hinged doors open, the alternatives were a folding strut, coil springs or torsion bars. Triumph had ruled out the use of a visible strut, and coil springs were found not to be of sufficient strength, while torsion bars as used in the estate were not viable due to the weight that would need to be supported.

The car survives at the time of writing, and it is displayed at classic car events from time to time. Opinions about the car by Triumph enthusiasts are mixed; in the eyes of some, perhaps the majority, it is an opportunity missed by Triumph, but to others, it is a styling abomination.

The vents under the rear window peak are visible in this view. The crisp styling of the car is also shown to good effect.

Revisions to the interior included relocation of the heater controls, a new style of steering wheel with chrome horn ring and the addition of fresh air vents, although some press reports mentioned that the location of the vents meant that the cool air was focused on the driver's hand and not onto the face. The dashboard is now a single colour.

The prototype fastback Triumph 2000 showing the unique rear styling that predated the market for large executive hatchback cars, such as the Rover SD1, by many years.

A huge glazed tailgate is a feature of the 2000 fastback. In the prototype, it is now supported by a heavy-duty mechanical strut; if such a car were to be designed today, gas struts would almost certainly be specified. The restricted loading area compared to the full-blown estate is obvious, although such a restriction has not impaired the ability of similar designs to sell today.

Although the market for estate cars in the mid-1960s remained a rather specialist market, Triumph's new model performed remarkably well in establishing the market for estate cars that provided a unique combination of comfort performance and load carrying capacity. Elsewhere in the market, estate cars remained rather utilitarian, and the arch competitor to the Triumph in the form of the Rover 2000 was not offered as an estate model, although a conversion was supplied by Panelcraft, but at significant additional cost with limited load hauling capacity. While the Triumph estate looked as though it had been designed from the outset in conjunction with the saloon, the P6 conversion had the appearance of a grafted on conversion and few were sold.

Elsewhere, the Ford Motor Company had responded to the market for 'executive' cars with the Corsair, a car heavily influenced by the current model Cortina and replacing the Consul Classic range that had achieved little success in the market. Both Corsair and Cortina were available as estate cars; the Cortina being rather utilitarian despite some models being offered with *faux* wooden panelling in a style aping that which was popular for a short time in the United States. The Corsair, while being a European design, featured frontal styling influences from the US-built Ford Thunderbird, and an estate model was

More typical of the estate car during the 1960s is this Vauxhall Victor. (Clive Wilkin)

Panelcraft created this estate version of the Rover P6. The car shown is a later 3500, but the body shell is fundamentally the same as the earlier 2000 model. The steeply sloping rear roof of the Rover did not lend itself to an estate conversion as easily as the Triumph.

provided by way of a conversion by Abbott of Farnham. Consequently, the finished model was expensive and when fitted with Ford's V4 engine fell far short of the refinement offered by the Triumph. The Vauxhall range included estate version of the Victor, and the Rootes organisation provided an estate version of their Humber Hawk. The Humber, while finished to a high level remained a traditional vehicle, complete with split tailgate, and compared to the Triumph 2000 estate, was from a different era.

5

Petrol Injection: A First for Triumph

The purchase of Standard-Triumph by Leyland Motors had been a good investment. With a newly revised model range and an image of 'sportiness', the brand was in the ascendant with models that were sought after and respected both at home and abroad. Supplanting the Standard name with Triumph had, indeed, been a 'Triumph'. The smaller Herald car and its associated performance derivative, the Vitesse, continued in production as did the small Spitfire and fastback GT6; all based on similar underpinnings had a loyal following then as they continue to have today. In 1966, a new model was introduced featuring a similar style to the 2000 and intended as a replacement for the Herald, which had now been in production for seven years. Adopting technology that was becoming widely adopted worldwide in motorcar design, this model was to be front wheel drive, and the only Triumph engineered car to use that form of transmission. This car, designed as Project Ajax, was launched as the Triumph 1300 with a body shell clearly influenced by the 2000 design and utilising the 1296cc engine from the Spitfire and Herald. Whereas the rival BMC combine utilised engines fitted transversely in their front wheel drive designs, the Triumph engine was fitted longitudinally. Although intended to supplant the Herald, the car proved to be successful in its own right in a market segment between the Herald and 2000. The Herald would thus remain in production into the future while the 1300 would itself donate its general body design to a further model range in the future with the resurrection of the Dolomite model name.

Across Warwickshire in Solihull, Rover enhanced their Rover 2000 by an important introduction in 1966 of the Rover 2000TC. Changes to the engine included a higher compression cylinder head and new manifolds, and fuelling was by a pair of SU HD8s. Overall, performance increased to a claimed 124 bhp, the 0–60 mph timing was reduced to 11 seconds and top speed increased to 112 mph. Furthermore, work on a rumoured 3-litre, six-cylinder engined version of the P6 was ended when Rover's Managing Director William Martin-Hurst was introduced to a Buick V8 engine design while on a trip to the United States. Manufacturing rights for Rover were soon negotiated, and production swiftly commenced. The first installation was into the stately Rover P5 saloon, much favoured as government transport prior to installation into the P6 body shell in 1968 to create the P6B, marketed as the 'Rover Three Thousand Five'. With a capacity of 3528cc (215 cubic inches) and an overall length almost identical to the existing four-cylinder engine, the all-aluminium engine weighed just 12 pounds more, and relocating the battery into the boot compensated for the marginal increase in nose weight thus retaining the weight distribution. With a substantial increase in power came an increase in top speed to 117 mph and 0–60 mph acceleration time of 9.5 seconds.

Not wishing to be left behind in the power and performance stakes, Triumph had been reviewing performance enhancements for their 2000. The car had developed some history in endurance rallying for which purpose the engine was equipped with triple Weber carburettors, producing power output in the region of 150 bhp. This came at the expense of a narrow power band, excessive fuel consumption and unacceptable noise and refinement for normal road use. But, it did demonstrate that the six-cylinder engine had room for power enhancements. Most pressing at the time for Triumph, though, was a replacement for the venerable four-cylinder wet liner engine dating back to the early 1950s Vanguard and still used in the TR4A sports car. Testing showed that the six-cylinder engine could be accommodated comfortably under Michelotti's elegant bonnet design of the TR4, but even in the higher state of tune as used in the GT6, the power output was still inadequate. Environmental pressures were also beginning to encroach on car manufacturers, and the need to limit emissions was becoming important. To meet the desire for more power, greater efficiency and corresponding lower emissions, Triumph turned to a new petrol injection (PI) system developed by Lucas.

Testing quickly showed that power output levels previously only seen with highly developed competition engines could be obtained with the new PI and did not need the race style cam profiles to achieve the required output, thus making the cars tractable and easy to drive in the real world rather than the arcane competition environment. It looked to be a promising development, but testing showed that low engine speed torque was lacking. To overcome this, the piston stroke was increased, giving an engine capacity now increased to 2,498cc. In perfect tune, the new engine delivered substantial increase in power, now up to 150 bhp, relaxed drivability and acceptable economy. The TR4A was transformed into the TR5, and the marketing department made much of this being the first British volume produced car to be fitted with PI. The technology hitherto being restricted to Grand Prix racing cars and exotic foreign brands sold at substantially higher prices.

The PI engine rapidly made its way into the 2000 saloon where it became the Triumph 2.5PI when announced in October 1968. With a slightly milder camshaft profile better suited to an executive saloon, power output was reduced to 132 bhp, still an increase of over one-third on the 2000cc model.

The Lucas PI system had its origins in military applications, and adaptations to the mass market brought with it a number of compromises that would come to light in a negative manner in future years. Instead of carburettors, fuel is provided to the engine through an injector nozzle per cylinder, each injector being mounted in one of three throttle bodies that replace the inlet manifold. Each throttle body has a pair of butterfly flaps that admit combustion air to the engine. For smooth running and optimal performance, it is essential that the butterflies are correctly balanced with particular care being taken to ensure that at partial openings equal volumes of air flow to each cylinder. Fuel is delivered to each injector under pressure from a metering unit constructed as a sleeve valve with multiple ports and an integrated shuttle. The rotation of the sleeve determines which injectors have fuel delivered, and its lateral position determines the quantity of fuel to be delivered.

The executive car market moved into a higher gear with the introduction of the 2.5PI, something that was reflected in the marketing brochure for the new car showing businessmen arriving for meetings and later departing to take a helicopter to the next important meeting. (©BMIHT)

The injectors, being purely mechanical, open automatically at a preset pressure. Engine vacuum, operating through a complex cam arrangement that in turn offsets the sleeve within the metering unit, controls the volume of fuel to be injected. Parameters such as air temperature or ambient pressure are not considered, and it can be seen that for the system to operate correctly, the overall health of the engine is important to ensure that the correct vacuum is developed to accurately dispense the fuel. Fuel is delivered to the metering unit by way of a high-pressure pump and regulator situated at the rear of the car adjacent to the fuel tank. The fuel pump itself was developed from that most widely used Lucas component – the windscreen wiper motor. However, despite its humble origins, correctly maintained and adjusted, the original pump has shown itself capable of a long and reliable life. Cold starting was undertaken in the same manner as a normally carburetted car as far as the driver was concerned. A 'choke' control operated an excess fuel device on the metering unit and, in conjunction, opened the butterflies a little to provide the combustion characteristics required to start from cold.

Despite a remarkable increase in performance, the Lucas PI system soon ran into trouble and tarnished the reputation not just of the 2.5PI and TR that employed the system, but of Triumph in general. Provided that the engine was in good order, the system would work fine, and problems with the car were rarely, if ever, related to the injection system even though common informed wisdom of the time suggested otherwise. It was essential that a thoroughly methodical fault-finding and set-up procedure was followed in diagnosing running problems with the car, particularly ensuring that valve clearances were correct and engine timing was to specification before condemning the injection. The electrical wiring to the fuel pump as designed was marginal when new, dirt or corrosion of the connections just making matters worse. It quickly became the normal practice for the cars, when out of their warranty period, to condemn the injection system as the cause of poor running and excessive fuel consumption, leading to an after-market in conversions to twin carburettor installations for poorly PI cars. This was made quite simple as Triumph had taken the

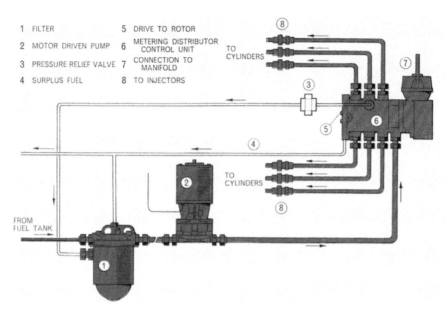

1 FILTER
2 MOTOR DRIVEN PUMP
3 PRESSURE RELIEF VALVE
4 SURPLUS FUEL
5 DRIVE TO ROTOR
6 METERING DISTRIBUTOR CONTROL UNIT
7 CONNECTION TO MANIFOLD
8 TO INJECTORS

TO CYLINDERS

TO CYLINDERS

FROM FUEL TANK

A general schematic of the Lucas petrol injection system extracted from a Triumph technical manual shows the major assemblies. (©BMIHT)

The inlet manifold and throttle arrangement on Triumph's implementation of the petrol injection system was complex with one throttle butterfly per cylinder, set within throttle bodies that were shared across two cylinders. A modern fuel system in contrast will use a single throttle to control the air supply to the engine. This configuration shows the throttle bodies with the air plenum removed and is from a TR, but the same general arrangement was used on TRs and 2.5PIs.

At an event celebrating the 50th birthday of the introduction of the big saloon, this 2.5PI is surrounded by other similar cars. The car appears to have wider than standard wheels, but standard Rostyle pattern hubcaps are fitted.

decision not to sell the PI system in the United States with the TR5 and later TR6 sold in that market with a conventional inlet manifold fitted with twin carburettors.

The late 1960s had been years of turmoil for the British motor industry. After acquiring Standard-Triumph, Leyland Motors also purchased the Rover business, along with their Alvis subsidiary. The BMC merger of the 1950s had expanded with the acquisition of Jaguar to form British Motor Holdings (BMH) and the government of the time under Prime Minister Harold Wilson encouraged the merger of Leyland Motors and BMH to form British Leyland. As is now well known, this was not to be the British motor industry's finest hour. Hugely inefficient and starved of new investment for decades, the British Leyland merger continued as though nothing had changed, other than a rearrangement of senior management. Harry Webster, Engineering Director for Triumph and undisputedly a key figure in Triumph's renaissance of the 1960s, found himself moved to the volume car division of Austin-Morris, the dealer network of which arguably should have been rationalised at the time of BMC's original creation. However, it now found itself competing further with its former 'enemies' of Rover, Jaguar and Triumph that were now part of the same business empire, and as if this was not enough, the industrial relations environment deteriorated rapidly as the economy continued to boom and bust.

Changes other than to the engine from the 2000 to the 2.5PI were slight, but significant. Braking remained as before with discs to the front and drums to the rear. The discs were thicker in section, and an uprated brake servo system was fitted. Tyres were 175 section radial as standard, and the wheels were fitted with a cover that replicated the 'Rostyle' design that was popular at the time and as fitted to the TR5. To fit the fuel pump into the boot, the revised design for spare wheel location under the boot boards was adopted as standard, and cosmetic changes were quite subtle. The rear 'C' pillar was covered in black vinyl and fitted with a circular PI badge, the boot lid was adorned with a 2.5PI badge and the air scoop on the bonnet wore a badge that proclaimed 'injection'. Inside the car, a sports steering wheel was adopted, but otherwise the interior remained the same as the 2000. And to cope with the increased electrical load, an alternator became a standard

PI cars were distinguished externally by a black vinyl covered C pillar fitted with a circular PI badge.

The bonnet of a PI car was embellished with a badge declaring the injection status of the engine underneath.

fixing. For the customer who needed to haul a larger load, a PI version of the estate was also offered.

According to the factory figures, the car was capable of covering the benchmark 0–60 mph acceleration in 10.5 seconds and to go on to a top speed of 110 mph, and the car would cost a new owner a few pennies under £1,488, including the now mandatory seat belts and purchase tax. Most owners would opt for either overdrive at an additional £65 or automatic at just less than £102.

Autocar road tested a car for a report published in their 6 February 1969 issue. The report begins with a description of a preview of the car in the form of a rally car developed for the 1967 RAC Rally that was cancelled due to an outbreak of foot-and-mouth disease. At the time, the preview was secret, but set expectations for the production car when it arrived. They said that they were '*impressed was an understatement; we raved about it, like all who tried it*', and on the test drive that consisted partly of hauling a family from London to Cornwall and back said, 'It is hard to describe the dynamic nature of the 2.5PI adequately; it is an eager car; the engine has that smooth song which makes six cylinders so much more refined than four.' The brakes came in for comment, being '*near perfect*', but inside the car, the heating and ventilation came in for criticism with the controls being difficult to use, the '*afterthought*' fresh air vents not allowing fresh air to reach the driver's face because it was deflected by the hands. They concluded their report by commenting that there is 'no doubt that this car has been designed for the enthusiast'.

Motoring Life took a 2.5PI and Rover 2000TC for a comparison, some six months later. An early observation was that the basic style of both cars had not changed in six years and compared that to the offering from Ford and Vauxhall concluding that '*neither has a chance against them*'. The Triumph won on interior comfort and the ability to carry five in comfort and in performance, finding it 'undeniably the faster and more effortless performer'.

Extracted from the original PI marketing brochure, the inside of the PI changed little from the lower-powered car. The only substantial change was to fit a more 'sporting' steering wheel. (©BMIHT)

One key customer group for Triumph expressed great interest in the 2.5PI. Many Police forces in the United Kingdom had evaluated the 2000 for use as a vehicle for both local policing and the more specialist traffic duties. The introduction of the 2.5PI became of great interest, and a number of such cars could be found in characteristic white and orange livery festooned with additional lights and deployed on the growing motorway network. It was in this role that some of the defects in the original implementation of PI system came to light, particularly fuel vaporisation. A feature of the system is that excess fuel is returned to the tank from the metering unit, and this fuel is at an elevated temperature as a result of under-bonnet temperatures and being pressurised. When the fuel tank is more than, say, a quarter full, the returned fuel will disperse its heat into the bulk supply, but as the tank empties, the ability to absorb the heat is reduced resulting in the temperature of the fuel increasing, the problem getting worse as the fuel level further reduces. Police duties would frequently consist of high-speed pursuits followed by periods parked at the side of the road, and it was in such circumstances that with a low fuel level, difficulties would be encountered with fuel vaporisation leading to cavitation of the fuel pump and the engine being unable to restart until fuel and pump had cooled adequately. Similarly, fast cornering with a low fuel level could lead to starvation with consequent air locking of the fuel system. Maintaining an adequate level of fuel in the tank would minimise the problem. Officially, Police specifications related to enhancements to the electrical system; many apocryphal stories abound of Police forces who retuned 2.5PI cars to TR5 specification, but no actual records can be found. With performance of two or three times that of the typical car of the era and handling to match, only a brave or foolish motorist would have decided to give a Police PI a run.

6

Project Innsbruck

The outcome of Project Innsbruck was the Triumph 2000 Mark 2. The major changes were restricted to new sheet metal front and rear and a new dashboard. This particular car was formerly owned by the Author and had previously experienced a very gentle life, being owned first by a firm of wedding photographers and then for twenty-eight years by a couple in Surrey. French Blue was a popular Triumph colour and suits the big car well.

With sales continuing strongly and acceptance in the market, it might be expected for the product planners at Canley to become complacent as had happened earlier with the one-time successful Vanguard, and the 2000 model range allowed to stagnate. This time, Triumph took a different approach and even before the new 2.5PI model was announced, plans were underway to replace the model with something new, keeping ahead of the rivals in Solihull, who confusingly would be part of the same company from 1967. Such was the bewildering state of the British motor industry in the 1960s and 1970s.

Money did not permit a bottom up redesign, but a refresh of the original design was to be undertaken. Triumph's primary design consultant Michelotti had been provided with a 2000 in connection with a design idea of his to create a Grand Touring Convertible to complement and compete with the market enjoyed by Mercedes with their SL range. The arrangement was that, in return, Triumph would receive first refusal on the new design for a model that could be a new range in its own right, or a possible replacement for the TR. The design study that required shortening the floor pan and creating a 2+2 convertible with many common points with the 2000 met with the full approval of Triumph and was to emerge in due course as the flagship of the Triumph range as the Stag. It, therefore, made perfect sense for the revisions to the 2000 model to incorporate the design of the new Stag, and for the various design cues to be incorporated into the remainder of the Triumph range where appropriate to create a harmonious and easily recognisable house style.

Triumph had already established a process whereby a 'new' model would emerge. The centre section of the car would remain and a new front and rear grafted on. This had already been applied to the TR range where, minor detailing apart, the last of the separate chassis TR cars, the TR6, shared the same centre section with the original Michelotti designed TR4. The same was to apply to the 2000.

Visually, the new Mark 2 saloon and Grand Tourer Stag show their commonality of design. Despite the similarities, neither the grille nor the lamp assemblies are interchangeable between the cars.

Above and below: Seen alongside each other, the longer bonnet and boot can be seen. The entire centre section of the car was retained.

Externally, little changed with the centre section of the car, the changes being limited to longer sections front and rear, both of which incorporated the design features being developed for the new Stag and looking totally up to date. The 'rocket cone' front was replaced with a cut-off, chrome-rimmed grille with the twin headlights retained and edged with indicator and marker light units. At the rear, the boot was lengthened providing a useful extra luggage capacity, but the lid now had an opening top only, meaning that luggage now needed to be loaded over a vertical rear panel. Rear lamps were arranged horizontally rather than vertically, as had been the case with the earlier models. On the saloon, the spare wheel was now standardised in its location centrally below the boot boards with hidden storage either side for carburetted cars and providing space for the PI apparatus on PI equipped cars. Mechanically, changes were quite minor; the rear track width was increased in common with the Stag requiring new semi-trailing arms and longer drive shafts. The front brakes used the thicker discs introduced with the PI models, and the rear drums gained a self-adjusting mechanism. Alternators were now a standard fitting.

Above and below: The earlier nose cone style perfectly captured the early space age era of 1963 when the car first came to market. The Mark 2 introduced a new squared off design, still with twin headlamps, now with the sidelights and turn signals at the outer extremities.

Above and below: The new car provided more luggage space, but at the cost of a higher loading sill to lift the luggage over. The spare wheel is now under the centre section of the boot floor with provision for the PI fuel pump and filters in a compartment alongside.

The new rear panel below the boot lid was finished with a black section on 2.5PI models. Rear lamp clusters on the Mark 2 are now horizontal.

The wiper motor derived fuel pump, filter and pressure regulator sit under the boot floor alongside the spare wheel. The relays and additional fusing are a later addition in an effort to overcome some of the weaknesses that were not uncommon in many cars of this era. (Colin Radford)

The effect of creating a new car was achieved with the overall appearance being of a new model despite the limited changes. Existing model names were retained with the suffix MK2 added to the name. Naturally, at this time, the outgoing model became known colloquially as the Mark 1.

PI models could be identified by the retention of the vinyl rear pillars and a black front grille, plus a new black vinyl adornment to the rear panel between the light assemblies.

The most significant changes were to be to the interior of the car, which was to be transformed. The genuine wood was retained, but a satin finish replaced the earlier high-gloss finish. Replacing the earlier dashboard was a modern wooden design featuring a large glove box, a centre section containing fresh air vents and an instrument panel containing all the instruments. A striking feature of this panel was a concave curved design that put the dials in clear view of the driver, and a centrally located 'all systems go' warning lamp cluster that had first been used on the earlier 1300, which would become a Triumph design feature. For the 2000 models, the instruments comprised a speedometer and combined cluster containing a fuel gauge, voltmeter and engine temperature gauge. On PI models, a tachometer replaced the cluster unit, and individual gauges were provided for the remaining functions. The overall design was harmonious with that to be used on the Stag when it was announced. Heating and ventilation was improved. The new heater, in common with the new Stag, was a very effective air blending type giving better control over the temperature of the heating air, and the location of the fresh air vents properly allowed the driver and front passenger to benefit from cold fresh air. Ducting to the rear of the car was retained to provide a supply of heating to rear passengers.

The top of the range 2.5PI could be identified by the matt black grille replacing the bright finished item on the 2000. The C pillars retained their vinyl finish and PI badges, and the rear number plate panel was also finished in black. (Paul Sheppard)

For many observers, the dashboard and instrument layout of the new 2000 were an improvement on the outgoing model. The overdrive switch is now in the centre of the gear knob, and all controls are in easy reach of the driver. Despite being over forty years old, the car illustrated still wears its protective plastic cover on the passenger door, the woodwork is undamaged by the sun and the car retains that familiar 'new car' smell.

The dashboard instruments were more comprehensive in the PI, in keeping with its more sporting pretensions. (Julian Wadsworth)

The steering column, which was now adjustable, featured twin stalk controls, one of which operated the turn signals, dip switch, horn and headlight flasher, while the other controlled the two-speed wipers, electric screen washer and flick wipe operation. Also on the steering column was located a rotary switch for the vehicle lights. This meant that other than a small rheostat to control the instrument lighting, the dashboard was completely clear of any switches, although in later years, the switch to operate the emergency hazard lights would be fitted to the dashboard. For cars fitted with overdrive, the operating switch was now a sliding switch let into the top of the gear knob; again a feature that became synonymous with Triumph even though it was not unique to the marque.

New door handles and window regulators were fitted. For the comfort of driver and passengers, either vinyl or brushed nylon seats could be specified. In what many saw as a retrograde step, the option for leather seating was dropped, but the quality of the vinyl used was such that it was and still is regularly mistaken for hide. Initially, the fabric covering was restricted to a centre section with the outer edges being vinyl and were later changed to an option of nylon cord material. The fitting of seat belts for driver and front passenger was now a legal requirement in the United Kingdom and many other countries, although the use was not to become compulsory until much later. To assist with the wearing and encourage the use of the belts, inertia belts were commonly fitted, and a transmission tunnel mounted buckle allowed for the belts to be secured single-handed.

A stalk on the right side of the steering column controls turn signals while that on the left works the wipers. A rotary switch on the steering column, which is adjustable for height, controls the vehicle's lights. This image also shows the 'Ambla' seating material, frequently mistaken for hide.

The more common cloth seating used a broad cord of nylon material. This material did not wear particularly well, and the rear seat on saloons was subject to damage by sunshine. Available in many colours, it does suit the overall style of the car very well. This later car is also fitted with headrests.

The estate car continued as before, but the cost of retooling to match the rear styling of the new car was considered too much, and so from the position of the C pillars rearwards remained in the earlier style, but with the new front and interior. This further complicated body shell assembly in that full Mark 2 bodies were built for saloon models, but the original rear panel assemblies were retained for the estate models, which continued to be completed by Carbodies. With the earlier body shell being shorter in both front and rear, this led to a unique feature of the Mark 2 model in that the estate car was dimensionally shorter than its saloon car origins.

Under the bonnet, the most obvious change was the fitting of a new cylinder head to the 2000 model derived from that fitted to the PI. To the relief of many motoring journalists who had previously commented on the heavy steering of the earlier model, especially when fitted with radial tyres, the option of power-assisted steering was now available. Wheel-rim width was increased to 5 inches with embellishment determined by the particular model. PI cars continued to be fitted with the Rostyle trims, while 2000 models wore simpler pressings in the style of a black and chrome flower head, sometimes referred to as 'sunflower' trims.

Motor were suitably impressed when they tested a 2.5PI MK2 in October 1969; they said that the changes uplifted it 'from a comfortable but staid looking car with a hot rod engine into a sumptuous well planned family sports saloon' that, they said, compared well with the

Above and below: With the Mark 2 estate, the new lengthened front and interior was matched to the original rear. The rear lights were retained, as was the styling of the rear wheel arch that was subtly different to the Mark 2. Like many Triumph estate cars, this example is fitted with a tow bar and is still used to tow a large caravan, a task to which these cars were and still are well suited.

Under the bonnet, things stayed much the same. At some point in its life, this car has had its original Zenith-Stromberg carburettors replaced with a set of SU carbs, but it retains the correct air cleaners and cylinder head. On this car, an AC alternator has been fitted from new, rather than the more usual Lucas item.

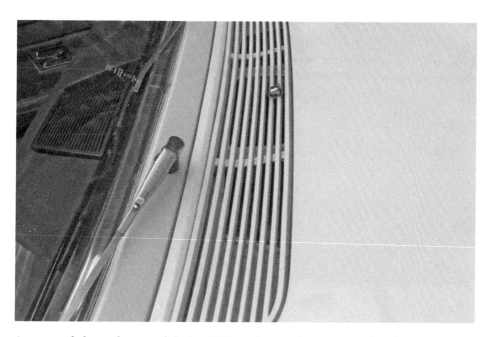

An unusual change happened during 1972. Earlier Mark 2 cars were fitted with an intake grille for the heater as shown here with slats that ran the width of the grille and reflected the style of the front grille, although finished in body colour. Later cars reverted to the Mark 1 grille with the slats running longitudinally as can be seen in the top image. The pressing to accommodate the bonnet catch of the Mark 1 was retained, even though the bonnet catch on the Mark 2 was relocated onto the bulkhead.

Under the bonnet, the PI installation did not change. The throttle bodies can be seen in the top image, with the six injectors fitted on top, one for each cylinder with combustion air fed through the large cylindrical air plenum. The lower image shows that on the other side of the engine, the metering unit below and behind the distributor and alongside the radiator, there is a vacuum reservoir to enhance the power assistance provided to the brakes. (Colin Radford)

BMW 2500 of the same era. An interesting comparison. The new option of power steering was seen as a worthwhile extra, not surprising as earlier reviews had commented on the 'he man' effort required at low speed. *Autosport* tested an automatic PI in January 1970 and concluded it was 'Britain's best medium sized car'. *Autocar* looked at a PI estate in July 1972 and compared it with two alternatives that were competitive in terms of luxury and performance. These were the Volvo 145E and Toyota Crown 2600, all three of which were priced at around £2,200 with the Triumph being in the middle of the range. The Triumph was highlighted for the refined trim, the 'restrained but luxurious interior styling' and its power and smoothness. It also commented that perhaps the reason that Rover did not offer an estate version of the P6 was that the Triumph was 'as well finished as its stablemates from Solihull and in terms of refinement falls between the [Rover] 2000 and 3500 V8'. The conclusion was that it was 'rather plush for a working car' and would be ideal transport for a family that were looking for 'a combination of utility, performance and handling'.

Industrial disruption notwithstanding the cars sold well and continued as a beacon of quality and sophistication among the British Leyland product range that was rapidly deteriorating and losing market share. The PI system, however, rapidly enhanced its reputation for being troublesome. An element of consolidation had occurred in the dealer network following the British Leyland formation, and now Triumph cars could find themselves being serviced and maintained alongside less-sophisticated Morris models.

Showing the earlier style of cloth seat trim, the interior of this 2.5PI looks like it has just been delivered to the supplying dealer. The seat-belt buckles were designed to be fitted with a single hand, buckling into a receptacle fitted between the front seats. (Colin Radford)

Above and below: Coupled with a period caravan, it is difficult to determine whether these images were produced in 1972 or more recently. This 2.5PI estate is still used by its owner for what it was designed: long journeys hauling a heavy load in comfort and at speed. The 2.5PI estate was probably the ultimate tow car with ample power and torque matched to a short rear overhang. The only downside being that if the performance was utilised, visits to a filling station could become very frequent. (David Rachel)

With the injection system requiring a different approach to fault finding and rectification, and with money not being available for proper dealer training, it became very easy for the unfamiliar injection system to be blamed for faults that existed elsewhere under the bonnet, not helped by mechanics unfamiliar with the aerospace levels of tolerance and adjustment necessary when setting up the system.

When correctly set up, PI systems would deliver the design specification of superior power combined with fuel economy; it was not uncommon to see PI cars, both 2.5PIs and TR6s emitting thick clouds of black smoke and unburnt fuel fumes while returning single digit fuel-economy figures. Some years after the PI system was ended by Triumph, the issues relating to poor performance became more widely understood, and a correctly set up PI system today in a classic Triumph can now easily deliver as designed.

With the new cars continuing to sell well, there was little need to apply changes to what was seen as a winning formula. With the upheaval in the motor industry of the time, the financial resource to do so was also lacking. That is not to say that changes were completely eschewed; one of the first modifications was the standardisation of a front anti-roll bar on estate models that had been found to suffer from excessive body roll when driven unladen. This became a standard fitting from the middle of 1970, while the following year, the prop shaft configuration was altered by the fitting of a new nose piece to the differential assembly. This had the desirable effect of reducing the various angles through which the universal joints were required to operate, reducing both wear and drive train vibration.

By 1971, the Press were beginning to compare Canley-built Triumphs with Munich-built BMWs. BMWs were rapidly climbing from near obliteration just a few years earlier to challenge the market that had so successfully been developed by Triumph and Rover. In April 1971, the magazine *CAR* undertook a Giant Test between a Triumph, a Rover and a BMW. Contrasting the list price of £1,867 for both the Triumph 2.5PI and Rover 2000TC with the BMW 2002 at £1,874, the first observation of *CAR* was that the BMW was lacking in 'the air of luxury' offered by the British-built pair, but said that the BMW more than compensated in performance and handling 'the other half of the appeal of these so-called executive saloons'. However, the overall conclusion was that the Triumph would be considered for its 'comfort, quietness and easy performance', and that the Rover delivers similarly other than its engine which 'can be tiresome after a while' before finally settling for the 'rather plain BMW 2002'.

Other detail changes were applied in an effort to provide some level of standardisation across the entire Triumph product range. As an example in late 1972, a new model overdrive was fitted in common with the TR6 requiring gearbox revisions. For the 1974 model year, the models were given a facelift with the result that, visually, the big saloons more closely resembled the range topping Stag that by now had been on sale for over three years. Externally, the most obvious changes were made to the front grille that changed from metal to a finned plastic assembly, and the front and rear bumpers gained a black rubber moulding to absorb minor parking grazes. Suspension modifications also resulted in a slightly increased ride height. Model names changed a little at this time with the 2000 ultimately having a TC suffix to its name, although not for a year after the 'facelift' model was introduced and the 2.5PI becoming the Triumph 2500 Injection.

Both cars had seen changes to their engines. In the case of the 2000, SU carburettors replaced the original Zenith-Stromberg units, and a new cam was specified while the

Inside the main assembly hall at Canley, saloons and estates are being assembled. (©BMIHT)

injected car was similarly fitted with a different cam, modified throttle bodies fitted with a revised linkage and a recalibrated metering unit, changes that were introduced in parallel with similar modifications to the TR6. The effect of which was to reduce the power to 120 bhp, down from 132 bhp, although the new figure was measured to the then current DIN specification.

A new model was also announced: the Triumph 2500. Power for this car was essentially the PI engine, but fuelled by carburettors. Power was just short of 100 bhp, fitting neatly between the 2000TC and injected cars and appealing to the customer who desired a little more power than was previously on offer from the carburetted car, but without the worry of the PI system. The 1974 model 2500 cars were badged simply as 2500 and were fitted with smaller carburettors. In May 1975, the model name and badging changed to 2500TC. For 1974, all three models were available as saloon or estate versions; deliveries of 2500 Injection estates ended in December 1974, having been on the market for just seven months.

Above and below: Two examples of early Triumph 2500 saloons. Apart from the engine, other visible changes include the 2500 badge on the C pillar and a black rubber strip now fitted to the chrome bumpers. The radiator grille now consists of wider spaced slats, the badge says simply '2500' in a new font, and inside the car, head rests are now available. (Paul Barlow – top and Bill Reed – lower)

Another early 2500 showing the detail of the front badge.

With the facelift, the badging of the PI was also changed. This badge is on a facelifted PI car that has been rebuilt to a very high standard as a historic rally car. (Lee Sellars)

The year 1975 saw a further rationalisation of the product, July seeing the final PI car being produced just a few weeks after the announcement of the model that was to crown the big saloon range for Triumph, the Triumph 2500S. Now boasting 106 bhp, fitted with a front anti-roll bar on both saloon and estate and with overdrive a standard fit on manual transmission models, the new model was equipped with five-spoke alloy wheels and became the final iteration in a range first introduced twelve years earlier. The interior was fitted with a sports-style steering wheel to control the standard power steering, and a full set of instrumentation in the style of the PI cars was fitted. Green tinted 'Sundym' glass, an optional extra, but widely specified, completed the image of a seriously upmarket, powerful executive express. With the introduction of the 2500S estate, production of the 2000 and 2500 estates also came to an end, making the luxurious, range topping 2500S estate the only estate car offered by Triumph.

In December 1975, *What Car* undertook a three-car test selecting a Triumph 2000TC, Vauxhall VX4/90 and Chrysler 2-litre. Overall, the Triumph came out on top, despite it being the oldest design and, marginally, the most expensive. The Vauxhall was described as '*a tarted-up Victor*', the Chrysler as attempting to 'out-Japanese the Japanese' because of the use of fake wood and quilted material for the interior. Contrast that with the thoughts about the Triumph's interior, which they thought was 'light years ahead' and it being 'old-fashioned in the nicest possible way' with instruments clearly placed and easy to read. Overall, it was the Triumph that was the pick of the three, finally commenting that most sales would be to loyal existing Triumph owners trading up with little or no advertising for a model that at the time was expected to be replaced the following year.

The ultimate version of the big Triumph saloon was the 2500S, a model that was marketed on its luxurious finish and performance. This example is an automatic and fitted with 'Sundym' glass and new alloy wheels, something that Triumph was fitting to several of their models, including Dolomite Sprints and Stags. Cars in the 1970s were finished in a series of bright colours of which this yellow is a good example.

Some of the PI features were carried over, including the black vinyl C pillars, now with an S badge, and the black rear panel below the boot lid. Another original and unrestored car, this car has been owned almost from new and for many years was the owner's everyday car.

Like many 2500S cars, this is an automatic, by now Triumph had replaced the Borg-Warner 35 series with the newer BW-65 model. A comprehensive set of instruments is fitted, but there are a few subtle differences when compared with the earlier PI. The dials now have a chrome rim, and the needles on the minor gauges now point upwards. A 'fasten belts' lamp has been fitted to remind the driver and front passenger to buckle up, and a hazard warning light system is now standard. With standard power steering, a smaller steering wheel is now provided.

The 2500S eventually became the only estate in the Triumph range. Within the British Leyland empire, other estate vehicles were offered such as the technically simple Morris Marina and technically interesting vehicles like the Austin Maxi that offered a five-speed transmission, a hatchback and cavernous load space. Perhaps for once, the management could see that it made sense to rationalise the product range with the Triumph estate crowning the BL range and not competing among other in-house products.

Saloon versions of the TC models continued until the end of production and by now sported a radiator badge that announced the fitting of twin carburettors. This particular car dates from just before the end of production and is finished in a typical 1970s shade of brown. The interior has been enhanced with the fitting of more modern seats, which are visible through the windscreen. Notice that BL's comprehensive new car warranty, branded as 'Supercover', is advertised by a sticker in the windscreen.

The 2000 models also eventually gained 2000TC badges. Both TC models retained the simpler instruments as fitted to the earlier 2000, but the 2500TC had a more 'sporting' steering wheel of the type fitted to the PI and 2500S, the 2000TC retaining the original style to the end of production. This particular example is an extremely well-travelled car seen here overlooking the harbour at Monte Carlo in 2011 when approaching thirty-five years of age. The car is in remarkably original condition despite having covered a substantial mileage in its life and is still used to tow a caravan.

Further rationalisation within British Leyland had seen former rivals Rover and Triumph in the same grouping as Jaguar. Perhaps as part of the same group, but customer loyalties were long lasting, and the potential for overlapping product ranges had to be eliminated. The big Triumph and Rover P6 had competed alongside each other since their introduction, with the higher-end models in both ranges biting at the heels of Jaguar. Rationalisation came with the replacement model planned for both the Triumph and Rover. With Triumph's reputation for producing cars with a sporting nature and past success in rallying as well as at Le Mans, the reasoning that saw Triumph focusing on smaller cars with sporting ambitions while Rover focused on larger, more luxurious offerings might have made sense, and Jaguar continued with development of their own product in the higher market segments. Rover and Triumph found themselves as British Leyland's new Specialist Division and plans called for two new models: one to replace the big Triumph and Rover P6, and the other, a smaller car to replace the Triumph Dolomite range. The latter product was cancelled, but the former was to emerge as the new Rover 3500, frequently known by its development code of SD1 (Specialist Division 1). It may have been a Rover in name, but Triumph technology was to be found in the gearbox, which was a Triumph design and in the six-cylinder 2600 and 2300 models. This six-cylinder engine was based on the now rather ancient Triumph motor, but now fitted with an overhead cam. A new Rover 2000 was a later product, but powered by a four-cylinder British Leyland O series engine.

The new Rover 3500 was launched in June 1976, overlapping slightly with the end of big Triumph production coming during 1977 after a production run of 14 years and over 315,000 cars. Triumph continued to build cars after the ending of the 2500S with Dolomite, Spitfire and TR7/TR8 production continuing just into the next decade. The final car model to bear the Triumph name was neither built at a traditional Triumph plant, nor was it a Triumph design, but it was a saloon car. The year 1981 saw the announcement of the Triumph Acclaim, a car based on the Japanese Honda Ballade but assembled in the United Kingdom with sufficient local content to justify the car as being locally built. Despite not being considered a 'true Triumph' by marque enthusiasts, the car was well received in the marketplace at the time, sold in volume and cemented in place a long-lasting and successful collaboration between the Rover Group, as the former British Leyland empire now called itself, and Honda.

7

Variations on a Theme

From the early production days of the 2000, Triumph was successful in marketing the big saloon to the local Police forces of the United Kingdom, and with the introduction of the 2.5PI, large numbers of white Triumphs adorned with additional lights, orange stripes and Police logos could be seen patrolling the growing motorway network. This was to be continued with the introduction of the MK2 car where PIs would continue in the fast patrol and pursuit duties, and lower-performance cars would be engaged on other duties. Particularly in the Metropolitan Police Service in London, a large fleet of 2500s were employed on numerous duties from diplomatic protection to local area response cars, often in unfamiliar colours for the Police, such as Carmine Red, Sienna Brown and Sapphire

Not quite as it appears, this Police liveried PI is not making enquiries, but is attending a classic car holiday weekend. The later style wheels are incorrect; they should be plain steel wheels with simple hubcaps, but the general appearance is representative of what would be seen patrolling motorways and in pursuit during the 1970s. (Alan Crussell)

Blue, and fitted with roof-mounted spotlights. Numerous additional options were available on cars to be engaged in law enforcement duties: calibrated additional speedometers from the era prior to advanced radar devices being very common along with uprated electrical systems to deal with the requirements of warning lights, sirens and radio systems. A roof lining fitted with a zipper is always a clue that the car had started life as a Police vehicle – the zipper making it easier to access the additional wiring for roof lights, etc. Many Forces specified simple hubcaps for the wheel, because it had been found that the trims fitted as standard were prone to flying off in high-speed pursuits. At least one Force also specified an automatic transmission selector that was limited to Park – Reverse – Neutral – Drive settings. Apocryphal stories abound of enthusiastic drivers using the automatic selector as a clutchless manual and overshooting the drive position with subsequent damage to the engine and transmission bringing an early end to the pursuit.

In the mainstream market, two low-volume variations were built. One such variation combined Triumph Stag mechanical assemblies with saloon and estate body shells to create a higher performance and even more luxuriously trimmed special model, and the other combined the car with the Ferguson four-wheel drive system.

With most former Police vehicles covering a substantial mileage and regularly being exposed to risk, it is not surprising that few genuine former Police vehicles survive. The Metropolitan Police retain a historic vehicle collection, including a Triumph 2500 injection that was registered at least a year after the final car had been produced. Model makers also liked the Police version of the car; the original of this Vanguard model will be familiar to transgressors of the law in London.

More Power and More Luxury

With the range topping GT model, the Triumph Stag being derived from the 2000, it was not surprising that consideration had been given to producing a new top-of-the-range saloon that might have been called Triumph 3000, taking advantage of the new V8 overhead cam engine developed for use in the Stag. Indeed, various saloons had been used as development tools for the Stag mechanicals, and while very little trim was to be interchangeable between the big saloon and GT car, despite outward appearances, fitting the V8 engine was not overly difficult. The shortcomings of the Stag engine and the utter turmoil within the volume model ranges of British Leyland that were to deprive Triumph of investment meant that the 3-litre saloon was never to be launched.

In retrospect, a Triumph 3000 would have been unlikely to create new business for the parent company; it would have just diverted sales from Rover and Jaguar. The enterprising owner of Atlantic Garages, 'Del' Lines a Triumph dealer in Weston-super-Mare, Somerset, saw a niche market opportunity for a car giving performance, comfort and carrying capacity. There was nothing in the market in the early 1970s that offered such a combination, other than the Reliant Scimitar or top-of-the-range versions of the Citroën Safari.

A factory-built 'special' version of a PI and allegedly built for a VIP in the Leyland company, this recently restored 'Triumph 3000' is seen on show at a classic car show. The 2000 structure was used as a development 'mule' in connection with the Rover SD1 for testing the 2600cc overhead cam engine that had been developed from the earlier Triumph unit. (Colin Radford)

Proving the concept by fitting a spare V8 engine into the shell of a 2000 with a defective motor, the project was moved forward by building a demonstrator model from a PI estate car. Mechanically, apart from fitting the Stag engine and transmission, the rear subframe was modified to allow a Stag-style exhaust system to be fitted and various under-bonnet modifications were required to allow the ancillaries to be fitted. A Stag-type battery tray was fitted behind the right-hand headlamps, and new engine mounts were required. At the rear, the arches were flared substantially to allow for wider wheels to be fitted. Internally, new Recaro seats replaced the originals, electric windows and sunroof were installed, and a new roof lining in black replaced that fitted by Triumph. The car was finished in Tartan Red, the colour worn previously by the BMC competition department cars and finished with a black vinyl roof – the height of motoring fashion and sophistication in the 1970s. With the detail of the car matching that of the Stag, the cars were named 'Stag saloons' and 'Stag estates', and the demonstrator was tested by *Motor* magazine correspondent Gordon Bruce whose subsequent report was extremely positive, considering it as coming close to his ideal car.

The concept was to be successful and orders for cars were received, typically from business owners with a loyalty to Triumph who were looking for a higher level of performance and comfort. Production cars were built from major mechanical components obtained from Triumph, many of which were warranty return items that were rectified where necessary, and body shells were ordered directly from the factory before being modified to accept the Stag-styling features. Much of the trim was sourced from scrap yards, giving rise to various anomalies with older trim items being used. Relations between Lines and the factory

The prototype 'Stag Estate' survives and has been subject to a thorough restoration by an enthusiastic owner. Shown here in a stylised photograph at a club event. (Jamie Furnell)

The body shell of the former 2.5PI estate was modified to accommodate Stag features such as the side repeater lamps. A Stag badge is fitted to the early PI style grille, in keeping with the age of the original car.

At the rear, badges highlighted the V8 engine of 3-litres capacity. Both were BL parts – the V8 badge being widely used and the 3-litre badge being the same as fitted to the slow-selling Austin 3-litre.

One of the two Stag saloons believed to have survived, and this car is undeniably a Stag saloon according to its official registration documents.

The chromed heater grille is also a Stag design motif, as is the coachline, and the front wing turn signal repeater can clearly be seen. Sundym glass and a top tinted windscreen add to the luxury of the car. Predating the option of air-conditioning, at least on UK cars, a full-length sunroof is fitted in the black vinyl covered roof making an eye-catching car with a very distinctive V8 exhaust note.

Every two years, one of the major Triumph clubs organises an event in homage to an earlier Triumph publicity stunt where cars would be driven 2000 miles around the United Kingdom non-stop to prove their reliability. Now run as a fund-raising event for charity, the event is hugely over-subscribed and early entry is needed to secure a place. In 2012, this Stag saloon is seen passing Sixpenny Handley in Dorset as it approaches the end of the event that had started 45 hours earlier in North London before visiting John O'Groats, central Wales and Land's End before returning to its starting point.

were to sour with a legal case over the use of the 'Stag' trademark being threatened and difficulties put in place concerning the supply of body shells. Undeterred, conversions of existing cars continued, but not without considerable extra cost.

Production continued until 1975, by which time twenty-two estate cars had been delivered and three saloons, all built as new cars with another saloon being assembled and first registered in around 1980. Of these, it is believed that three estate cars and two saloons have survived, all of which were built as new cars.

More Grip and Safety

Harry Ferguson, the industrialist best known for his tractor and agricultural machinery interests, had a long involvement with the Standard Motor Company through an agreement in the 1950s with Sir John Black to build the eponymous 'little grey Fergie' tractors. That relationship proved very lucrative to Standard, although relationships between Sir John Black, Chairman of the Standard Motor Company and Harry Ferguson were often acrimonious as summed up by Colin Fraser in his biography of Ferguson (*Harry Ferguson: Inventor and Pioneer*): 'Both men were inflexible and aggressively certain that their opinions were infallibly right.' Ferguson was a colourful character who, among his other claims to fame, could count the accolade for being the first person in Britain to build and fly his own aircraft. His developments in mechanising agriculture and especially the three-point linkage made Ferguson a household name, but his interest in all-wheel drive systems are of interest here in connection with Triumph cars.

All-wheel drive systems have been in use since before the 1914–18 War, but generally limited to use on soft surfaces. In the same way that a differential is required between wheels on the same axle to accommodate the different turning speeds of wheels while negotiating a bend, an all-wheel drive system needs to allow for differences in rotation between axles if it is to be used on hard surfaces without causing drive shafts to lock up with subsequent risk of failure. If a system could be developed that allowed for an automatically locking central differential, Ferguson believed that this would provide a step forward for road going cars by enhancing their road holding and therefore safety.

To this end, in the 1950s, Ferguson, in association with business partners Tom Rolt and Freddie Dixon, both successful names in period motor sport, developed a family car design that incorporated both the full-time four-wheel drive system and anti-lock brakes. The resulting design was shown to several of Britain's motor manufacturers with a view to engaging their interest in either building Ferguson's design alongside their own product or incorporating the design features into their own product. Ferguson's robust personality, coupled with the high costs that would be incurred, meant that the negotiations were not successful, but in 1960, following Ferguson's death, his son-in-law Tony Sheldon became the Chairman of the company with the new intention of developing a four-wheel drive system that could fit existing production cars.

The challenge in the design was to create a differential unit that could lock and unlock automatically and smoothly to ensure that the power was distributed to the wheels with the best adhesion. The company, now known as FF Developments, originally developed two types of mechanical centre differentials, and both required extremely tight engineering tolerances and therefore were expensive to manufacture. The first model was used in the only four-wheel drive Grand Prix car to achieve a win, driven by Sir Stirling Moss at Aintree in 1961. The second model was the type used in the Jensen FF. The breakthrough came when a silicon-based oil became available that had the interesting property of becoming more viscous as it became warmer, contrary to the characteristic of most oils. Here was the beginning of the viscous control unit of the type now widely used in full-time four-wheel drive systems with the advantages of being cheap to manufacture and able to continuously vary the torque transmitted to the two axles. Designed by FFD, the system was to be manufactured by the company of GKN-Birfield.

Five Triumph cars were to be fitted with the FFD system: two of which were Stags, two 'big' Triumph Estates, one of which was fitted with a Stag engine, and one saloon. Fitting of the four-wheel drive system required the engine to be raised, resulting in a bulge to the bonnet and for the transmission tunnel to be widened. Both estate cars survive in 2016, restored and maintained to a high standard.

Both estate cars that were fitted with the Ferguson FFD system have survived. This particular example, fitted with a Stag 3-litre V8 engine is shown on a trailer immediately following a comprehensive rebuild from a condition that many said made the car completely unrestorable. To accommodate the engine, which was raised to provide clearance for the four-wheel drive unit, the bonnet has been reshaped to give the appearance of the earlier style fitted to the Mark 1 model. (Colin Radford)

Looking under the bonnet, the Stag engine fits neatly into the available space even though it has been raised for clearance underneath.

The 2.5PI engined FFD estate car was built for a customer in Switzerland where the car remains. Again, it was necessary to raise the engine, and a modified bonnet accommodates this. The all-wheel drive system works so well that the car has been used in recent years to rescue more modern vehicles that have become stuck in the Swiss snow. (Bill Munro)

PI engine installation in the FFD car. (Bill Munro)

Underneath the car, the transfer box can be clearly seen positioned at the rear of the Borg-Warner 35 automatic gearbox. From here, the drive is taken rearwards to a conventional differential and forwards to an additional differential and drive shaft arrangement at the front axle. (Bill Munro)

8

A Triumph in Motor Sport

From the introduction of the TR range, Triumph had success in rallying as well as at Le Mans, and the rallying success continued into the 1960s with an easily recognisable team of light blue TR4s. It had become increasingly apparent that the structure of rallying was changing with a need for a more robust vehicle, particularly for the longer endurance events that were becoming part of the rally scene. With some development, the 2000 was seen as being ideal for this type of sport. Built as Group 3 entries allowing for a degree of modification, the power output was enhanced to 150 bhp using triple Weber carburettors matched to a re-profiled high lift cam and careful selection of gear ratios with overdrive on all but bottom gear that resulted in seven evenly spaced ratios. A limited slip differential and 15-inch TR4 wheels delivered the power to the ground. Externally, the cars were finished in white with blue roofs and a matt black bonnet. The first Works entry for the 2000 team was to be the 1964 Spa-Sofia-Liege event that was to show up the weakness in the rear suspension attachment causing all three cars to retire in Yugoslavia, but not before first showing the capabilities of the cars in such rough conditions. The RAC followed on with team drivers Roy Fidler and Terry Hunter taking second and third places in their class.

Matching the style of the early Works Triumph 2000s, this example regularly competes in historic rallying and has a registration that is visually similar to those of the Works team. The original four Works cars were registered AHP 424B – 427B. (Colin Radford)

The year 1965 brought further class success in the Tulip Rally and RAC event, but in 1966, a change to the regulations presented the Triumph Works team management with a dilemma: either build and sell sufficient Group 3 cars to qualify for homologation, withdraw entirely from the sport or enter but in Class 1 for cars that were essentially normal production vehicles. One such car was driven in the Monte Carlo Rally by Roy Fidler finishing in 14th place overall, the other two cars entered failed to finish.

With this, Triumph withdrew Works support from motor racing, although the cars would continue to be entered privately in rallying. One of the former Works saloons found its way into saloon car racing driven by Bill Bradley backed unofficially by the factory and employing all round disc brakes and, interestingly, a PI 2-litre engine. Without full-blown Works support and funding, it was unlikely that the car would compete successfully against the contemporary BMW1800s and Lotus-Cortinas.

For the 1967 RAC Rally, two cars were prepared for Group 6, the prototype category. Pre-dating the 2.5PI, these cars were fitted with TR5 PI engines and were to be driven by Fidler and F1 champion Denny Hulme. Less than 24 hours before the scheduled start of the event, it was cancelled due to a widespread outbreak of foot-and-mouth disease. The 2.5PI rally cars would see success, but not for a few more years and then under the guise of British Leyland's Works team.

FHP 993C was driven by Works driver Roy Fidler with some success in 1966 and 1967. Fitted with a petrol injected engine, it was expected to do well in the 1967 RAC Rally, but this was not to be as an outbreak of foot-and-mouth disease led to a late cancellation of the event. The car still survives and is seen here on show at a classic car show on loan to one of the enthusiast's clubs. (Colin Radford)

The 1970 World Cup Rally captured the imagination of everyone with an interest in motor sport. The format for a long-distance marathon rally had been set in the late 1960s with the London-to-Sydney event, but this was to be by far the toughest motor sport event ever to be held. But first, three PI rally cars were to achieve a remarkable victory in the 1969 RAC Rally achieving first, second and third positions in class. Triumph's PR department naturally took advantage of the class success with an advertising campaign. These cars were to be shipped to South America where they became recce cars for the main event of 1970.

With the Works team now headquartered at the former BMC Works department at Abingdon, work began in earnest to develop the cars for the trip to Mexico. Outwardly similar to standard cars, the body shells were substantially strengthened and lightened with aluminium panels. Additional spare wheels were carried along with additional long-range fuel tanks. Four cars were entered as Works cars with two private entries. With the exception of entry number 88, registered XJB 305H and crewed by Brian Culcheth with his regular co-driver Johnstone Syer, the other entries would all consist of three men. Of the two private entries, one registered BYE 377H was of similar specification to the official cars with preparation by Janspeed. This car started the event with mechanical troubles and was to make front-page news at the start of the event when the driver, keen to make up lost time, was stopped by the Police for speeding.

The advertising department at Canley lost no time in turning the RAC Rally success to commercial advantage with this advertisement promoting the car as the first British saloon with petrol injection: 'Triumph put in what others leave out.' (©BMIHT)

Triumph show 'em a clean pair of wheels.
(1, 2, 3, in their class)

For this year's RAC International Rally the conditions were particularly swinish. The snow came thick and fast and early.

So did the dropouts. Less than half finished. Engines, transmissions, suspensions, and bodies took a real beating.

And storming in as one, two, three in their class—the Triumph 2.5 P.I.—the first British saloon with petrol injection as standard equipment.

If you needed proof of our statement 'Triumph put in what the others leave out', you've got it. In triplicate.

RAC INTERNATIONAL RALLY OF GREAT BRITAIN, 1969. CLASS 6. PRODUCTION TOURING CARS OVER 2,000cc.

1	**2**	**3**
Triumph 2.5 P.I. Andrew Cowan & Brian Coyle.	Triumph 2.5 P.I. Paddy Hopkirk & Tony Nash.	Triumph 2.5 P.I. Brian Culcheth & Johnstone Syer.

Three team cars started, three finished.
The best team performance by British Cars.
Results are subject to official confirmation.

TRIUMPH

WORKS ENTRIES			
Registration	**Rally No.**	**Driver**	**Co-Driver(s)**
XJB 302H	98	Paddy Hopkirk	Tony Nash, Neville Johnston
XJB 303H	92	Evan Green	Jack Murray, Hamish Cardno
XJB 304H	43	Andrew Cowan	Brian Coyle, Uldarico Ossio
XJB 305H	88	Brian Culcheth	Johnstone Syer

PRIVATE ENTRIES			
Registration	**Rally No.**	**Driver**	**Co-Driver(s)**
BYE 377H	1	Robert Buchanan-Michaelson	Roy Fidler, Jim Bullough
UKV 701H	39	Adrian Lloyd-Hirst	Keith Baker, Brian Englefield

The 'office' for Brian Culcheth and Johnstone Syer recreated with input on the detail from Brian and Johnstone. Overhead ventilators were necessary as the original fresh air intake between the bonnet and windscreen was used to provide combustion air for the engine. Fresh air is now supplied via an external roof-mounted vent, the cover of which was taken from a humble Morris JU250 van. Notice the toggle switch on the gear knob to operate the overdrive.

Above and below: A cosmetically faithful replica of Brian Culcheth's car has been recreated with Brian's input in getting the detail correct. The original XJB 305H was destroyed after a short career as a Works car and latterly as part of 'Brian Culcheth Team Castrol' competing in the 1971 Scottish Rally, an event that Brian had won in another 2.5PI in 1970, and the Welsh and Cyprus Rallies of the same year.

British Leyland Chairman Sir Donald Stokes was at the start of the event and made it clear that only outright victory would be acceptable. So no pressure on the entrants.

All the Works entered cars, along with one of the privateers, completed the European stages and were shipped to South America. The extremes of the environment took its toll on the cars: Lloyd-Hirst's car suffered suspension damage in Brazil that put it out of time; Evan Green's car suffered a terminal engine failure in Argentina, while Andrew Cowan's car was involved in a serious accident that was to see the car fall 20 feet to land on its roof destroying the car and putting its crew in hospital with serious injuries. The wreckage of the car was subsequently repatriated and rebuilt. Mechanical failures and damage affected the remaining cars of Culcheth and Hopkirk, but both were to finish in second and fourth places, respectively. Overall, a huge success for the Triumphs, but Stokes seemed to want better with the official Works competition department being closed once again in October 1970.

Competition with the big saloons did continue with entries in the East African Safari and Brian Culcheth's own successes with his own team cars. Eventually, Triumphs were to return as Works entries, but by then the car of choice would be the newer Dolomite and wedge bodied TR7/TR8. For many with an interest in sporting Triumphs, the World Cup Rally result, notwithstanding the lack of outright win, was the car's greatest achievement.

Brian Culcheth and Evan Green pose for a photograph at the start of the World Cup Rally at Wembley Stadium. (Brian Culcheth)

After Andrew Cowan's serious accident in XJB 304H, the wreckage was shipped back to Abingdon to satisfy the customs authorities. Subsequently rebuilt using a spare body shell that had been constructed to the same specification as the cars entered in the event, the car survives in the condition that it was built. In 2010, an event was held at what is now the British Motor Museum at Gaydon Warwickshire to celebrate the 40th anniversary of the rally where entry number 43 was to be a star attraction. The Ford Escort in the background is a replica of the winning car registered FEV 1H. The replica is registered H1 FEV.

A roadside service halt at Albi in France during the European stages of the World Cup Rally. Paddy Hopkirk's car is nearest to the camera with Brian Culcheth's in the centre. This image and those on the following page were taken by Mike Wood, one of the BL support team members. (Mike Wood)

Paddy Hopkirk's car has suffered some frontal bodywork damage along the route as can be seen in this image taken at one of the service points. Brian Culcheth's car had also suffered a little with a broken windscreen. Fortunately, a replacement windscreen was among the spares that had been deposited along the route. Unfortunately, it was found that the replacement screen was the wrong item. As ever, duct tape is the rally mechanic's friend. (Mike Wood)

Finally, at the end of the event in Mexico City, the damage to car 98 can be seen. (Mike Wood)

9

Triumph 2000: The Legacy

In 1963, the market for a 2-litre, four-door saloon car with sporting performance and styling that was attractive to an aspirational buyer did not exist. The choice was either a volume produced anonymous 1600cc car that no doubt achieved its design objectives of carrying up to four people and their luggage or a substantially larger and consequently more expensive 3-litre car targeted towards the company director. For the go-ahead middle manager, the gap in the market was profound. The Triumph 2000 and to a lesser extent its rival from Rover changed that situation at a stroke. Stylish, spacious, comfortable, affordable and different to anything else in the market, the new car defined a new market segment.

With the introduction of the 2000 estate, Triumph managed to create another market – everything that went before with the saloon was now available with additional luggage space for the weekend or during the week for business use. The introduction of PI – the first for a British-manufactured saloon car – was to significantly enhance the performance capabilities of the car, but not at the cost of any of its other attributes. And the 1969 introduction of the Mark 2 model was to achieve something that Triumph was a master at. To all intents, an altogether new car, yet one that was achieved within the cost restraints imposed by the parlous financial situation of the motor industry in general and British Leyland in particular, reusing all that was good in the outgoing model, but clothing it in a refreshingly new exterior that set a design statement for all Triumph cars. Until the end of production in 1977, the Triumph 2000 and 2500 models remained popular, stylish and respected motor cars.

Today, the aspiring business professional has a choice of cars, but two brands, both German, dominate the market created by Triumph: Audi and BMW. There is an irony in that BMW chose to retain the Triumph brand name and intellectual property when they disposed of their holding in what had become the Rover Group. Perhaps, this was in recognition of the contribution that Triumph had made in developing the market segment that BMW products now occupy? Perhaps, if the industrial landscape had been different, the car of choice today for an aspiring business executive would still wear a Triumph badge?

Perhaps if things within the British motor industry had been different in the 1960s and 1970s, this is the sort of car that Triumph might have produced as replacement for the 2.5PI? Certainly the spirit lives on and the market that is now dominated by BMW and Audi for fast, luxurious executive expresses can surely be said to have been created by Triumph with the introduction of the 2000 back in 1963?

Acknowledgements

Every attempt has been made to seek permission for copyright material used in this book. However, if we have inadvertently used copyright material without permission/ acknowledgement, we apologise, and we will make the necessary correction at the first opportunity.

Certain images used in this work have been taken from sales brochures and other material originally published by the manufacturers; they are acknowledged as the copyright of British Motor Industry Heritage Trust (BMIHT), © BMIHT. All publicity material and photographs originally produced for/by the British Leyland Motor Corporation, British Leyland Ltd and Rover Group, including all its subsidiary companies, is the copyright of BMIHT and is reproduced here with their permission. Permission to use images does not imply the assignment of copyright, and anyone wishing to reuse this material should contact BMIHT for permission to do so.

Everyone who I have approached for assistance in compiling this book has been without exception helpful. In particular, the Directors of the Triumph 2000 Register who have offered every assistance and helped with sourcing cars to photograph and in providing photographs from their own collections. Especially, I must single out Colin Radford who has helped with a large selection of his photographs, many of which have adorned the cover of the club magazine *SIXappeal* over the years. Andy Roberts, President of the Register, helped with information on the cars built by 'Del' Lines, and fellow author Bill Munro was very helpful with information on Carbodies Ltd, who built the estate cars, and on the Ferguson 4WD system. Tony Edgeworth, Matt Field, Dave Bullen and Mike Allam kindly indulged my requests to photograph their Triumphs in detail, and thanks to Brenda Griffin who now owns the very early 1963 Rover 2000, photographs of which are used to contrast the similarities in approach taken by both companies. All images in this book that are not otherwise acknowledged are my original work.

Triumph motor cars have been the source of many publications over the years, a good number of which have been written by former Triumph Competitions Secretary Graham Robson. These have proved to be very useful to check where my own memory had failed and needed to be refreshed. The 'Further Reading' list will allow the reader to expand on the detail contained herein, particularly in respect to the 1970 World Cup Rally.

Finally, I have to express my thanks to Ann who has put up with my irrational interest in Triumphs for many years.

Further Reading

Robson, Graham, *Works Triumphs in Detail* (Herridge & Sons, 2014).

Robson, Graham, *World Cup Rally 40* (Veloce, 2010).

Robson, Graham and Langworth, Richard, *Triumph Cars, The Complete Story* (MRP Publishing, 1979).

About the Author

Kevin Warrington has a long family connection with what is loosely called 'the motor trade' reaching back to the origins of mechanised road transport. However, he chose a career in the computer industry until redundancy in 2001 allowed him to indulge a passion for writing, photography and classic machinery in general.

With his wife Ann, he ran a specialist motor coach company for several years, operating a fleet of 1950s classic coaches used primarily for television productions and film work as well as for wedding hire.

He is an occasional contributor of words and pictures to several classic transport magazines and has edited two Triumph club magazines: *TR Action* for the TR Register and *SIXappeal* for the Triumph 2000 / 2500 / 2.5 Register.